Junior NKIERE MAKOLONI

COMPUTER COURSE THIRD YEAR CG

Junior NKIERE MAKOLONI

COMPUTER COURSE THIRD YEAR CG

ScienciaScripts

Imprint
Any brand names and product names mentioned in this book are subject to trademark, brand or patent protection and are trademarks or registered trademarks of their respective holders. The use of brand names, product names, common names, trade names, product descriptions etc. even without a particular marking in this work is in no way to be construed to mean that such names may be regarded as unrestricted in respect of trademark and brand protection legislation and could thus be used by anyone.

Cover image: www.ingimage.com

This book is a translation from the original published under ISBN 978-620-6-72074-4.

Publisher:
Sciencia Scripts
is a trademark of
Dodo Books Indian Ocean Ltd. and OmniScriptum S.R.L publishing group

120 High Road, East Finchley, London, N2 9ED, United Kingdom
Str. Armeneasca 28/1, office 1, Chisinau MD-2012, Republic of Moldova, Europe
Printed at: see last page
ISBN: 978-620-8-05761-9

PREFACE

National and international initiatives have had an impact on many educational sectors. The growth of the IT industry has led to a steady increase in the number of specialists in this sector and, in turn, to the rapid development of specific training courses in secondary and higher education and the use of IT in all subjects. At the same time, the development of IT has given rise to new systems of representation, new skills, new roles for both teachers and pupils, the decompartmentalisation of educational institutions and new frameworks beyond the formal school environment and existing teachers (Voogt & Knezek, 2008).

SUMMARY

Every day, customer demands and expectations reach new heights, slowing down the demand for digital and real-time services. As a result, modern companies are investing in digital transformation and business automation, which involves integrating various software solutions (SaaS) and cloud applications. With these systems, companies can digitise and automate business processes in marketing, sales, customer service, human resources and all other departments. These integrated systems are part of the company's integrated IT ecosystem.

However, with each new software solution a business integrates, managing these connections and exchanging which data is ultimately more and more difficult. In the absence of an appropriate platform to integrate all these systems, the benefits of digital transformation and business automation are overshadowed by a major problem: a tangled IT environment.

OBJECTIVE GENERAL

By the end of the third year of the business and management humanities, learners will be able to use IT tools to enter documents and solve complex accounting and financial problems.

SPECIFIC OBJECTIVES

At the end of this course, any student who has followed it assiduously will

will be able to :

- Learn more about text formatting and other word processing tools;
- Use the Internet for correspondence; ● Burn information to CD or DVD;
- Sort data in ascending or descending order according to set criteria;
- Filter data using the simple and personalised method; ● Present data graphically;
- Calculate the earned value and present value of compound interest and the annuity.

CHAPTER I

BASIC CONCEPTS (2)EME

I.1. SELECTION OF A TEXT

In Word, you can select all the text in a document (Ctrl+A), or select text or specific items in a table using the mouse or keyboard. You can also select text or elements located at different points. For example, you can select a paragraph on one page and a sentence on another.

Select all text

1. Click anywhere in the document.

2. Press Ctrl+A on your keyboard to select all the text in the document.

Select a specific text

You can also select a word, a line of text or one or more specific paragraphs.

1. Place your cursor in front of the first letter of the word, sentence or paragraphs you want to select.
2. Click and hold the mouse button as you drag the cursor to select the text you want.

Other ways of selecting text

To select a single word, quickly double-click on it.

To select a line of text, place your cursor at the start of the line, then press Shift+Down Arrow.

To select a paragraph, place your cursor at the start of the paragraph, then press Ctrl+Shift+Down arrow.

I.2. TEXT FORMAT (style, size, font, colour) Emphasis added)

I.2.1. CHANGE STYLE

You can modify a style directly in the Styles gallery, without using the text in your document.

1. In the **Home** tab, right-click on a style in the Styles gallery, then click **Edit**.

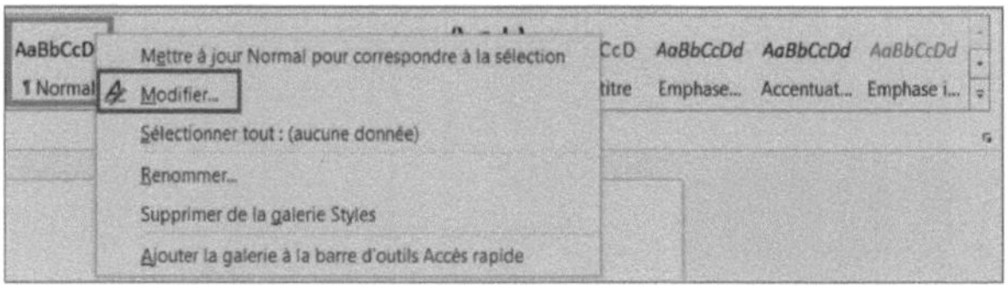

2. In the **Formatting** section, make the desired formatting changes (for example, font style, size or colour, alignment, line spacing or indentation).

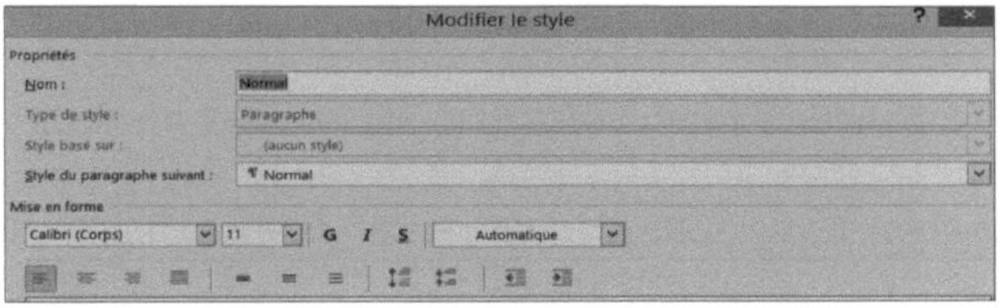

3. Indicate whether the style change should apply to the documentor all your future documents.

I.2.2. MODIFICATION OF SIZE

To change the font size of text selected in Excel, PowerPoint or Word :

1. Select the text or cells whose text you want to change. To select all the text in a Word document, press Ctrl +A.
2. On the **Home** tab, click on the font size in the

Font size .

You can also type any size you like in the following limits:

- Excel: between 1 and 409, between 1 and 409, in multiples of .5 (for example,

10.5 or 105.5)

- PowerPoint: between 1 and 3600, in multiples of .1 (for example, 10.3 or 105.7)
- Word: between 1 and 1638, in multiples of .5 (for example, 10.5 or 105.5)

Advice :

- When you select text, a mini-toolbar is displayed near your cursor. You can also change the size of the text in this toolbar

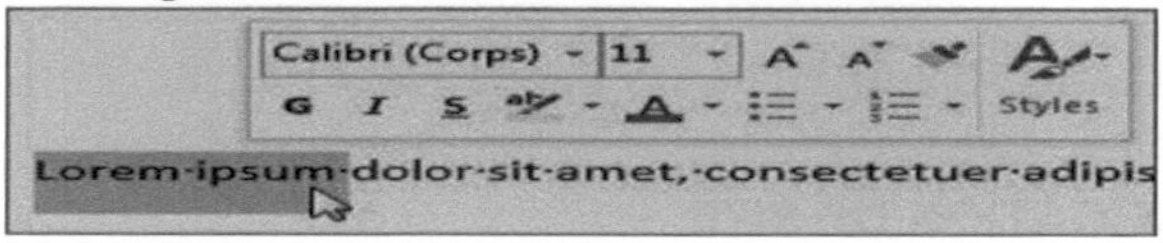

- You can also click on the **Increase** font size or **Decrease font size** icons (**Increase font** and **Decrease font** in some earlier versions of Office programs) until the desired size is displayed in the Font **size** area.

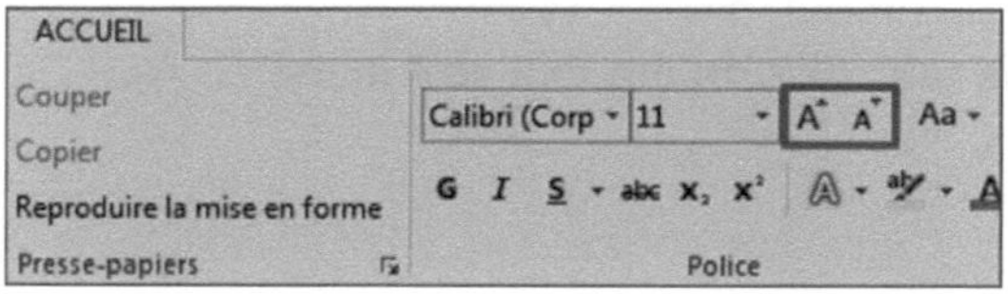

I.2.3. CHANGE THE COLOUR OF A TEXT

You can change the colour of the text in your Word document.

1. Select the text you want to change.

2. On the **Home** tab, in the **Font** group, select the arrow next to **Font colour**, then select a colour.

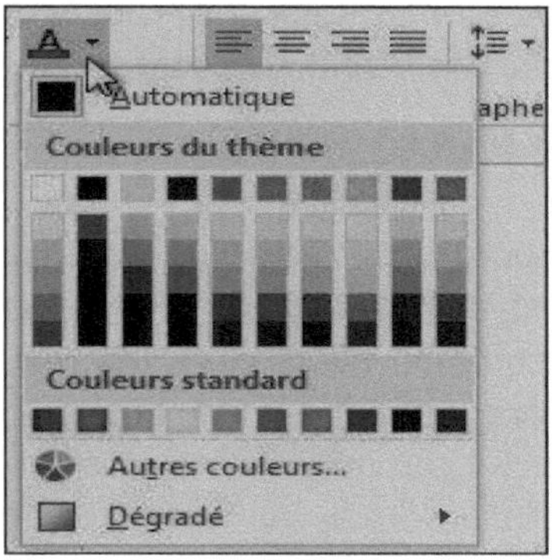

You can also use the formatting options in the mini-toolbar to quickly format text. The mini-toolbar is automatically displayed when you select text.

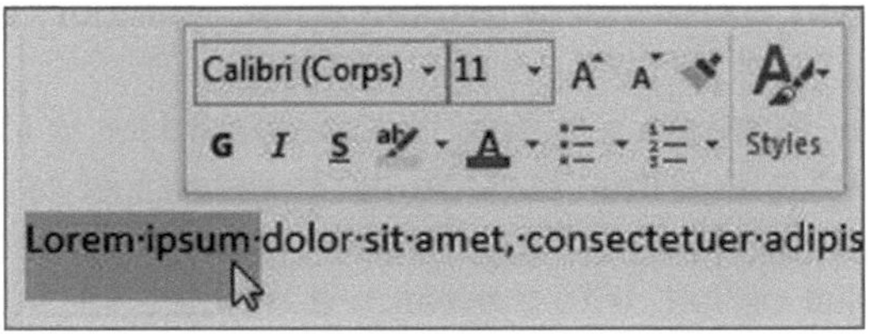

Advice :

- If you don't see the colour you want, select **Other colours**, then a colour from the **Standard** tab, or combine your own colour from the **Custom** tab.
- To change the colour, transparency and shadow of the text, select **Gradient**. The Gradient tool is not available in Word 2007.

I.2.4. UNDERLINE TEXT

To underline text, simply tap on the text you want to be underlined. Click and drag on the text you wish to be underlined to highlight your selection. Press the "CTRL" key and the "U" key on your keyboard at the same time. To stop underlining, press "CTRL" and "U" again. To underline using the Microsoft Word menus, click and drag under the text you want to be underlined to highlight your selection. Click on the "Home" tab on the left-hand side of the Ribbon. Click the "U or S" button on the left-hand side of the Ribbon under the "Font" category.

I.2.5. ALIGNMENT OF PARAGRAPHS

Text alignment is a paragraph formatting attribute that determines the appearance of the text in a paragraph. For example, in a left-aligned paragraph (the most common alignment), the text is aligned on the left margin. In a justified paragraph, the text is aligned on both margins.

①align text left;② centre text;③ align text right;④ justify text;⑤ distribute text

I.3. APPLICATION EXERCISES (Bulleted list, Number,..)

The easiest way to create a bulleted or numbered list is to enter the text for the list, select it, and then click on the Bulleted List or Numbered List buttons on the Control panel. These buttons can be used to activate and deactivate the list option or to transform a bulleted list into a numbered list and vice versa. You can also include bullet and number attributes in a paragraph style and generate a list by assigning a style to paragraphs.

Note:

Automatically generated bullet and number characters are not actually inserted into the text. As a result, they cannot be searched for using the text search function, nor can they be selected using the Text tool if they have not first been converted to text. Bullets and numbers also do not appear in the editor mode window (except in the paragraph style column).

To create a bullet or number list, do the following:

1. Select the paragraphs making up the list or click where you want the list to start to create an insertion point.
2. Use one of the following methods:

- Click the Bulleted List or Numbered List button in the Control panel (in Paragraph mode). While holding down the Alt key (Windows) or Option key (Mac OS), click a button to display the Bullets and Numbering dialog box;
- Choose the Bullets and Numbering command from the Paragraph panel or the Command panel. For List Type, choose Bullets or Numbers. Specify the required parameters, then click OK.
- Apply a paragraph style that includes bullets or numbers.

3. To continue the list in the next paragraph, move the point

to the end of the list and press Enter or Return.

To end the list (or a section of the list, if the list is to continue later in the article), click the Bulleted List or Numbered List button in the Control panel again, or choose the Bullets and Numbering command from the Paragraph panel menu.

I.4. NUMBERING OF PAGES

Numbering the pages of a Word document may be necessary in certain cases: for an academic paper, a text with a table of contents or any document that is a little bulky.

Page numbering is automatic in Word. As well as activating it, you can set a number of optional formatting parameters.

1. Click on the **Insert** tab.

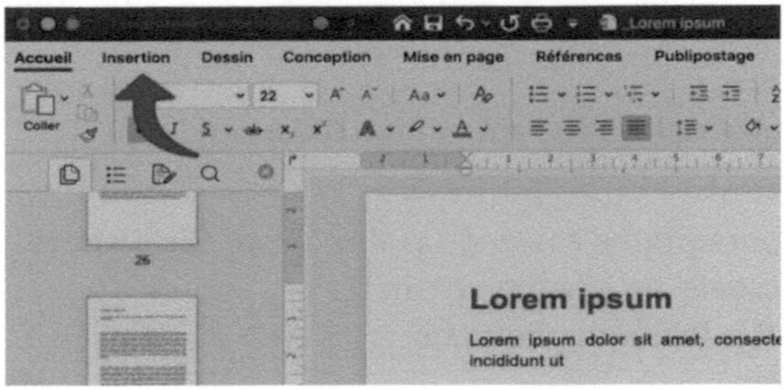

2. Click the **Page number** button. If it does not appear, resize the window to full screen.

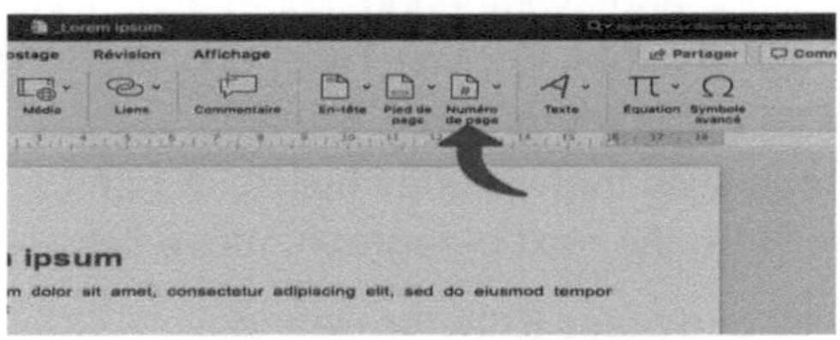

3. From the drop-down menu, select the **Page number** option.

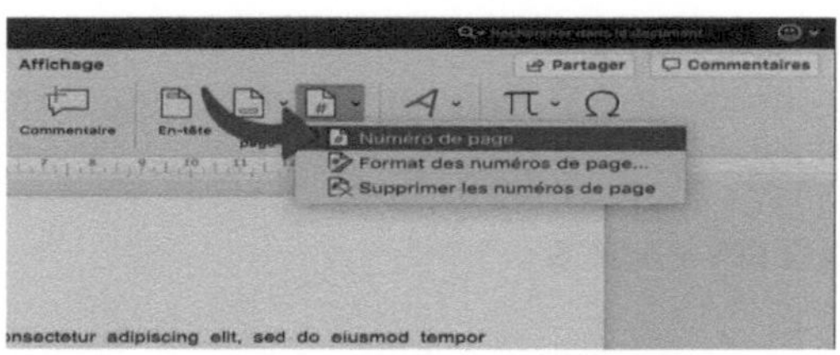

4. The window that opens lets you choose whether the page number will be displayed at the top or bottom of the page, as well as its alignment. Uncheck the **Start numbering on first page** box if you do not want the cover of the document to be numbered (it will still be taken into account). If you wish, click on the Format button. Otherwise, go directly to step 6.

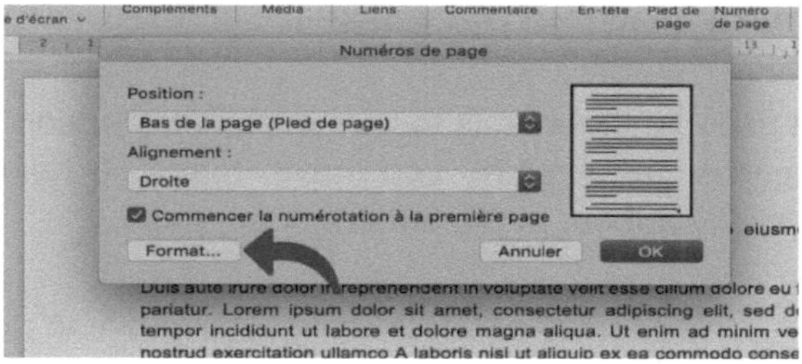

5. The **Page Number Format** window lets you change the pagination type and start numbering from any number greater than 1. When you have finished, click **OK.**

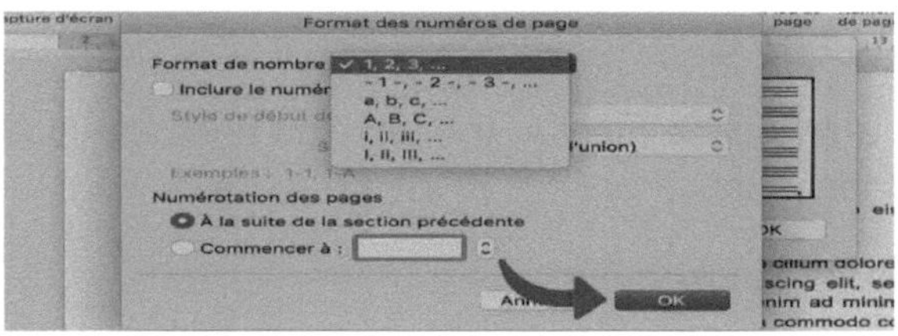

6. Click **OK** again to apply the changes.

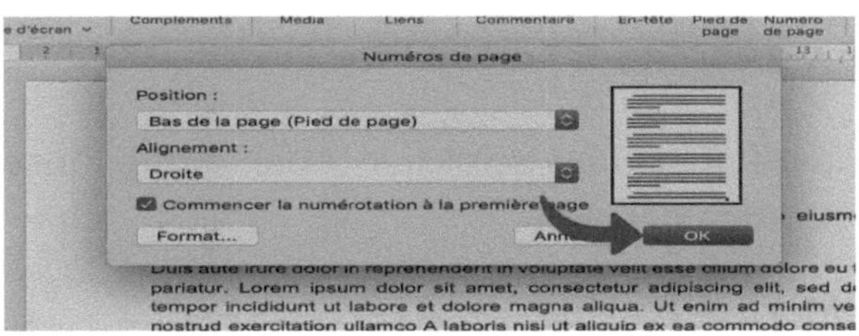

Page numbers complement the automatic table of contents. This automatically retrieves the titles of your chapters and lists them in an index placed at the beginning or end of your document.

I.5. INSERTION OF FOOTNOTES PAGE

Footnotes are used in documents to give explanations, add comments or provide references to a point you have made in your document. Footnotes generally appear at the bottom of the page.

To add a footnote, follow these steps :

1. Click where you want to add a footnote page.

2. Click on **References** > **Insert a footnote**.

Word inserts a reference mark in the text and adds the footnote mark at the bottom of the page.

3. Type the text of the footnote.

Tip: To return to where you were in the document, double-click on the footnote marker.

I.6. INSERT A GRAPHIC

To insert a simple graph from scratch in Word, click on **Insert** > **Graph**, then select the graph you want.

1. Click on **Insert** > **Graphic**.

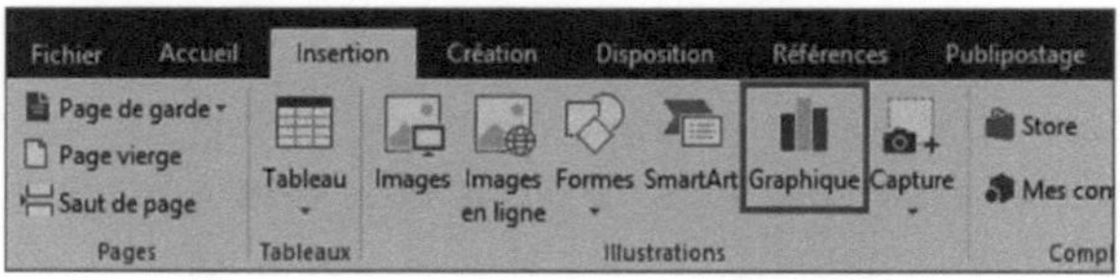

2. Click on the chart type, then double-click on the desired cart.

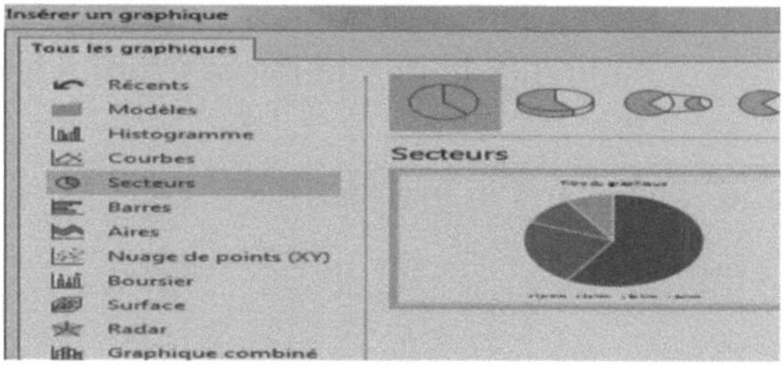

Tip: To help you choose the type of graph best suited to your data, see Available graph types.

3. In the spreadsheet that opens, replace the data with default with your information.

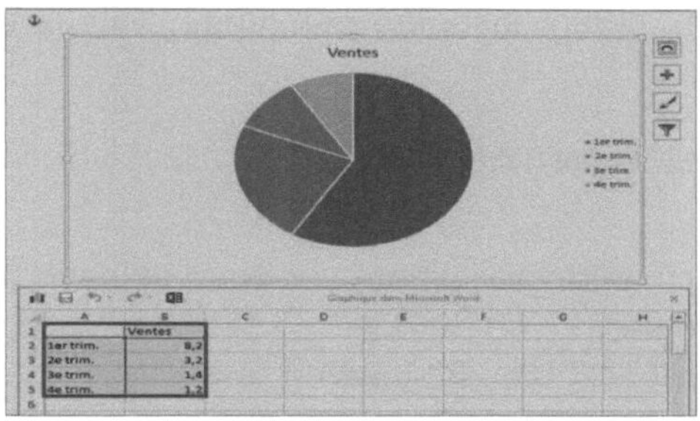

Tip: When you insert a graphic, small buttons appear in the top right-hand corner. Use the graphics button to display, hide or format elements such as

such as axis titles or data labels. You can also use **the** Chart styles **button** to quickly change the colour or style of the chart. The Filters **button**

graph is a more advanced option which displays or hides the data in your graph.

4. When you have finished, close the spreadsheet.

5. If you wish, use the **Options** button layout to organise the graphics and text in your document.

I.7. INSERT AN IMAGE

There are two ways of inserting an image into a Word document:

- using the "Image" command in the "INSERT" tab
- with click and drag

Tip!

Remember that the image you insert will always appear at the insertion point (the location in the document where the flashing insertion bar is). To avoid surprises, click in the document to place the insertion point where you want it, before inserting the image. This is where the image will appear.

METHOD 1: INSERTION TAB > IMAGE

1. In the Word document, click where you want to insert the image to place the insertion bar.
2. Click on the "INSERT" tab and then on "Images".

3. In the "Insert an image" dialogue box, locate the folder containing the image you want, click on the image to select it and then click on the "Insert" button.

METHOD 2: CLICK AND DRAG

If you need to insert several images, the click-and-drag method makes the task quicker and easier. First, put all the images in the same folder and proceed as follows:

1. In the Word document, click where you want to insert the image to place the insertion bar.
2. Open the folder containing the image.
3. Arrange the windows so that both the folder window and the Word document window are visible.
4. Click on the image and, holding down the mouse button, drag it onto your document

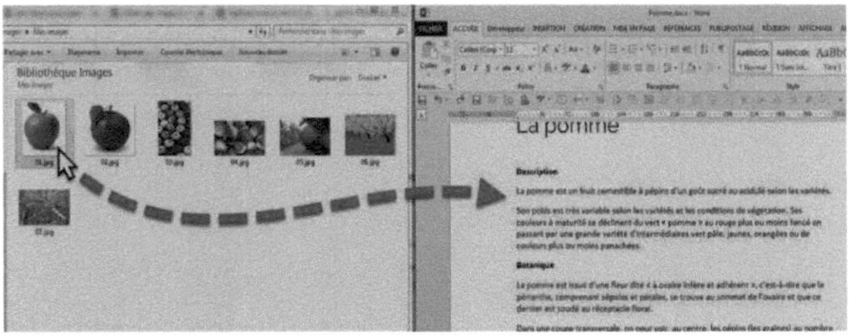

Images can be dragged from the desktop, from a window in an open folder (as above) or from another application (with exceptions). They can also be dragged between two Word documents.

I.8. CREATING COMPLEX TABLES

Word has a dedicated function that lets you create a table very easily. In your active Word document, click on the "Insert" tab and select the "Table" icon. Word then simply asks you to select the number of rows and columns you want for your table **directly with your cursor**. With one click, the software inserts the selected number of rows and columns into the document.

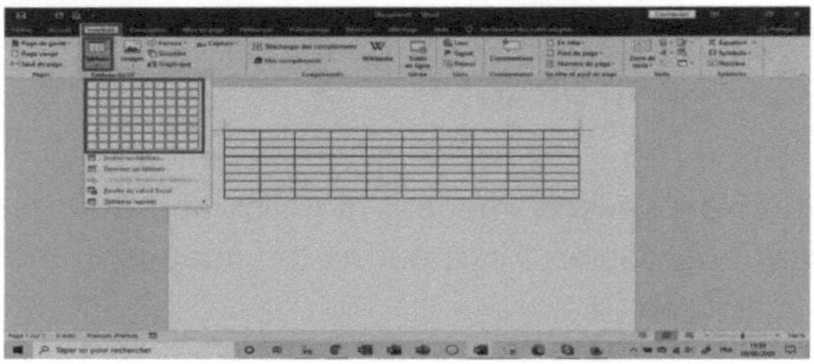

You can easily define the size of the table by moving the cursor over the grid.But there are also other ways of creating tables in Word, such as the 'Insert a table' option just below the grid. If you click on it, a dialogue box appears with various options that allow you to customise your table before creating it. First you specify the number of columns and rows. You can also define **the width of the columns**. You can set a fixed column width yourself or let Word set it automatically. The software then determines the width of the column according to the content or size of the window.

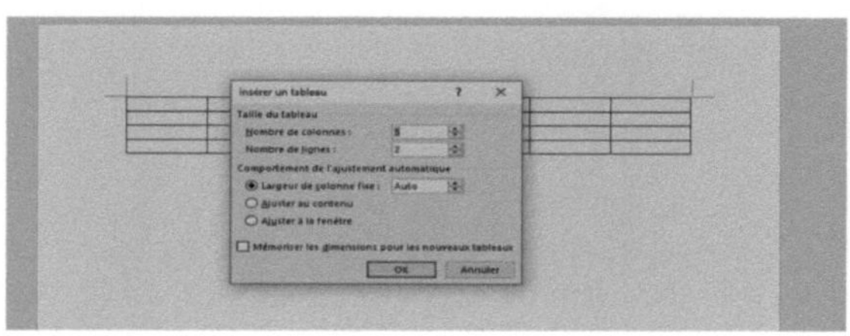

Please define the exact dimensions of the width of the columns in your table.There's another feature that lets you **draw tables**. You can draw a cell of any size, then add extra rows and columns to create your table step by step.

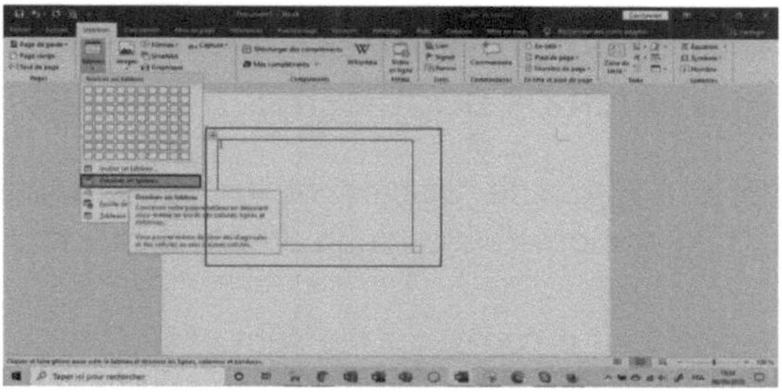

Use the cursor to draw a cell to make your table.

Good to know: if your **document already contains data to be processed**, there is a function that allows you to convert your data into a table. All you need to do is format your data beforehand by creating different lines for words or numbers and separating them with tabs. Word will then determine how to divide the content into rows and columns. Then select the text you want to convert and click on "Table" in the "Convert text to table..." menu. When the dialogue box opens, make sure that Word has correctly taken into account the division between columns and rows, then create your table.

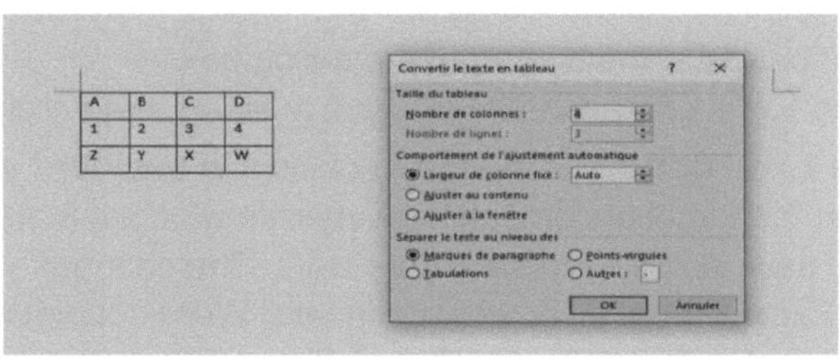

If your document already contains data, you can convert it directly into a Word table.

CHAPTER II

REMINDER OF DOCUMENTS ATTACHED

An attached file is a computer document that accompanies an e-mail message. It can take various forms, such as Word or Excel files, images, sounds, etc.[1]

It can also be defined as a computer file sent at the same time as an e-mail message. Attached documents are also known as[2] attachments.

II.1. CASE STUDY ON DOCUMENT ATTACHMENT (WORD, EXCEL.)

Using MS Word and Excel, you can link documents together by embedding them. Embedding an Excel document or file in a Word document means that you can see the Excel spreadsheet in the Word document, and any changes you make to the Excel file appear in the Word document. The same is true for Word documents linked to Excel documents.

1) Open your Word document and choose "Insert" from the menu bar, then "Object".
2) Select "Excel sheet" in the dialog box that opens, then click on the "Select a file" button at the bottom of the dialog box.
3) Choose the Excel spreadsheet you want to insert, then click "Insert".
4) To edit the Excel document, double-click on it in the Word document. This will open the Excel document in a separate window. Make your changes and save bothfiles to save your work. The changes you have made in the Excel file will also show up in your Word document.Inserting a Word document in Excel Spreadsheet ;

5) Open your Excel spreadsheet and choose "Insert" from the menu bar, then "Object";
6) Select "Word document" in the dialog box that opens, then click on the "Select a file" button at the bottom of the dialog box;
7) Choose the Word document you wish to insert, then click on "Insert";
8) To edit the Word document, double-click on it in the Excel document, in the same way as described above. Save your work in both files when you're finished. Once again, the changes you make in the Word

ocument will also appear in your Excel spreadsheet.

II.2. SEND A DOCUMENT ATTACHMENT

The procedure is the same for all webmails and email software.
To send an attached file, first create a new message, then click on the appropriate command (Attach or Attach a file) in the toolbar of your webmail or email software. You then need to browse your hard disk to select the file you want to send.

But the easiest way to attach a file to an email is to **drag the icon** of the document you want to send to your email inbox.
Note that when you attach a file to an e-mail, it is always preferable to mention this in the message itself.

II.3.RECEIPT OF ONE OR MORE DOCUMENTS ATTACHES(Download)

- In your web browser, once you've logged in to your Gmail account, in the list of messages in the **Inbox**, click on **the subject of the email** (and not on the attachment, even if it is visible just below the subject).

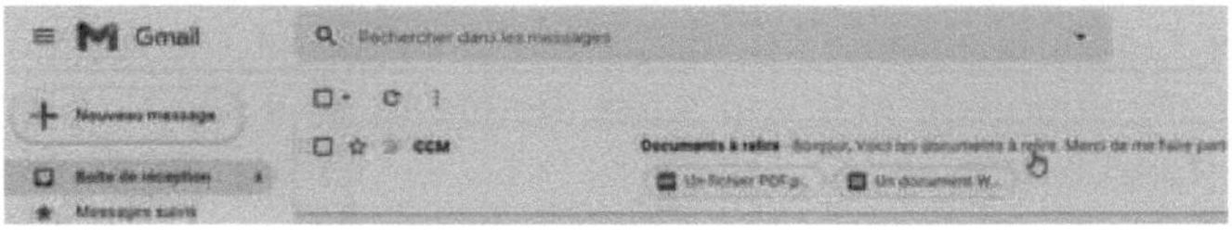

- In the e-mail, place the mouse pointer over the attachment you want to recover, **without clicking on it** (if you click on it, you will ask to see a preview of the file).
- The **Download** icon (representing a downward arrow) appears superimposed on the attachment: click on the **Download** icon.

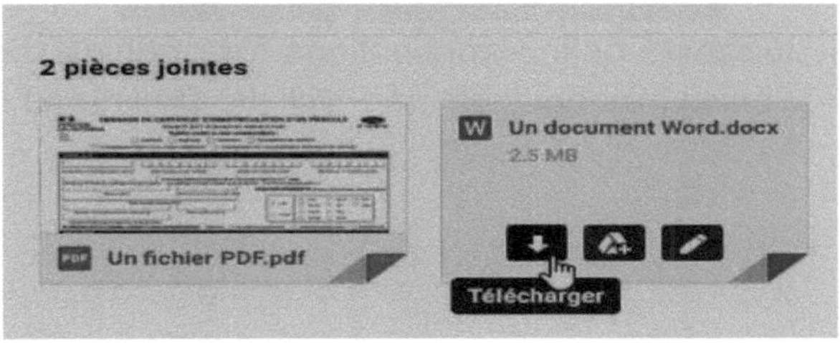

• What if you've clicked on the attachment but not on the **Download** button? No problem! You've just asked Gmail to show you a preview of the file. For example, press the **Escape** key or click on the **Close** icon at the top left of the window, which represents a left arrow. Or else.

• . Either Gmail displays a preview of the document received as an attachment, click on the **Download** button at the top right of the file preview window.

• . Either Gmail is unable to display a preview of the document and automatically suggests that you save the file to your hard drive: click on the **Download** button.

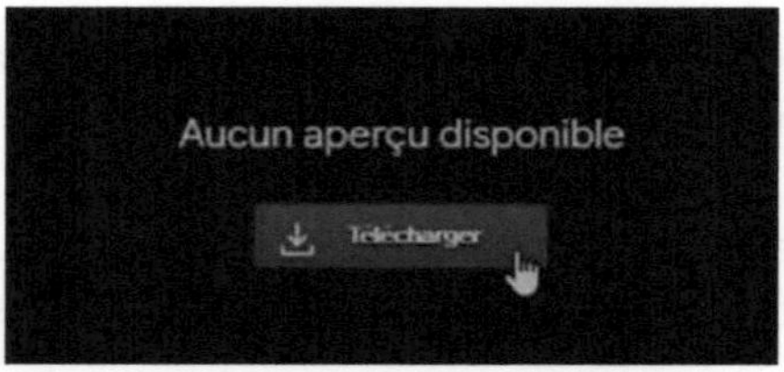

• . If Gmail suggests online applications for opening the document (see illustration below), ignore them and click the **Download** button.

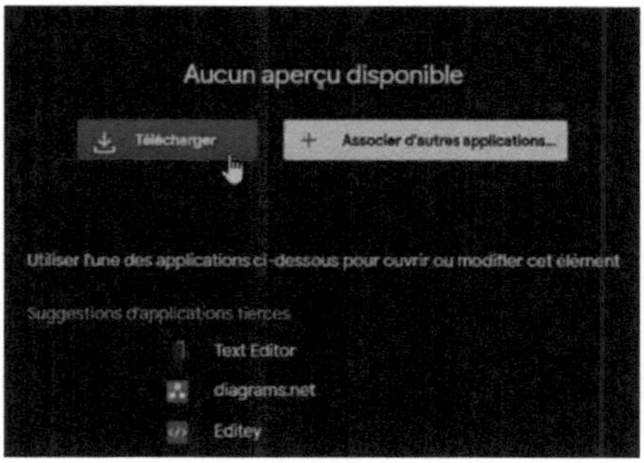

• Some browsers will download the attachment directly, while others will ask you to confirm the registration: all you have to do is accept, as shown below in Firefox for Windows.

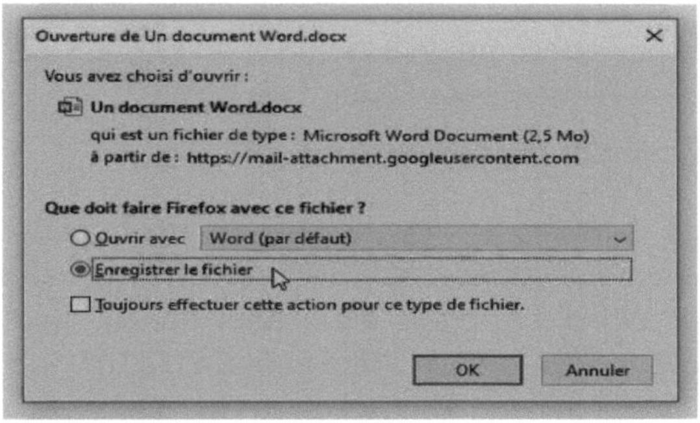

• The file is downloaded by your browser and can be found in your **Downloads** folder, both on Windows and Mac (at least if you haven't changed your browser options).

• If the name of the attached file ends in .zip, it is a compressed file and should be decompressed:

Note that if you're the sender of the message and the recipient hasn't replied to you, the email won't appear in your **Inbox**. But you can go to Gmail's **Sent Messages** folder, open your e-mail and download its attachments.

II.4. TAKING A PHOTO WITH A DIGITAL CAMERA

Digital cameras have become an essential part of our lives. They help us capture and preserve memories of our daily lives.

How does the camera capture an image?

A digital camera captures an image using an image sensor. The image sensor is an electronic device that converts the optical image into an electrical signal. When you press the shutter button, the camera opens its shutter, allowing light to enter the camera. This light is focused by the lens onto the image sensor, which converts it into an electrical signal. The electrical signal is then processed by the camera's image processor to form a digital image.

The different parts of a camera

A digital camera is made up of several componentswhich work together to capture and display an image. The lensis the most important part of the camera, focusing the light onto the image sensor. The image sensor is the electronic device that converts the optical image into an electrical signal. The shutter button controls the opening and closing of the camera shutter, allowing light to enter the camera. The image processor transforms the electrical signal into a digital image. The LCD screen displays the captured image.

How does digital photography transform an object into an image?

Digital photography transforms an object into an image by capturing the light reflected from the object and transforming it into a digital image. The image sensor captures the light and converts it into an electrical signal, which is then processed by the camera's image processor to form a digital image. The digital image can then be stored on a memory card or displayed on the camera's LCD screen.

The body responsible for restoring the image on the right side

The organ responsible for rendering the image on the right side is the brain. Our eyes see the world upside down, and it's the brain that corrects this orientation and makes it appear right side up. Similarly, when we look at an image on the LCD screen of a camera or on a computer screen, our brain processes it and turns it right side up.

So where is the image formed in the camera?

The image is formed in the camera's image sensor. The image sensor is a rectangular electronic device that captures light and converts it into an electrical signal. The image sensor is located behind the lens and is the most important part of the camera that captures the image.In conclusion, digital cameras capture an image using an image sensor that converts the optical image into an electrical signal. The image is then processed by the camera's image processor to form a digital image. The LCD screen displays the captured image and our brains put it back the right way round. Understanding how a digital camera captures and displays an image can help you take better pictures and appreciate the technology behind it.

II.5. RECOVERY ON THE MACHINE

After opening and viewing an attachment, you can choose to save it on the computer If a mail contains several attachments, you can save several attachments as a group or individually.

Here's how to register :

1. Click on the attachment in the reading pane or the open message.

2. On the **Attachments** tab, in the **Actions** group, click **Save As**. Alternatively, right-click on the attachment and click **Save As**. To select several attachments, hold down the Ctrl key.while selecting attachments. To save all the attachments, choose **Save all attachments**.

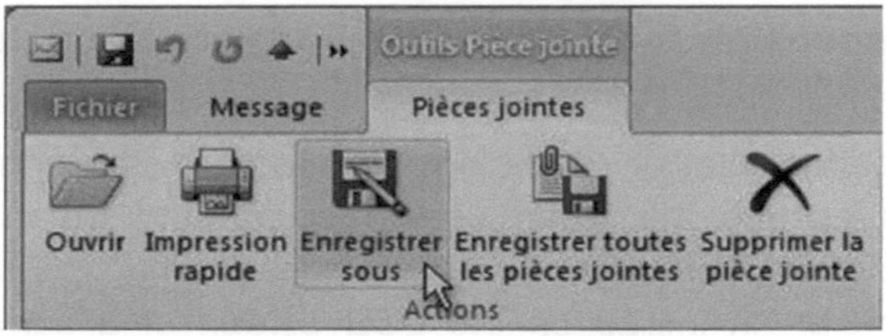

Note: If the mail is in RTF format, in the Reading pane or in Open mail, right-click on the attachment and then click **Save as**.

3. Click a folder location, then click **Save**.

II.6. SEND FILE ATTACHMENT

Stage 1

Select a message (this can be a received message or a new message by pressing the "Write" icon on your toolbar).

Step 2

If it's a received message, press the "Reply" or "Forward" button on the toolbar.

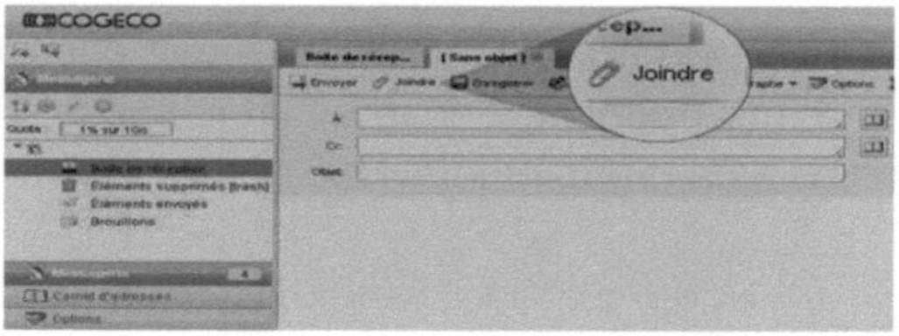

Step 3

Once the email is open, click on the "Attach" icon.

Step 4

Select the file you want to attach and click the "Open".

Step 5

Enter the address of the contact you wish to send the file to in the "To" field.

Step 6

Send the message.

II.7.ORGANIZING ELECTRONIC MESSAGES (Creating files)

To organise email messages, you need to create folders in which they will be managed. Here's how to create :

1. First, open Gmail on the web and click on the cogwheel icon in the top right-hand corner. Then click on "View all settings".
2. Next, go to "Inbox" and set the type of inbox to "Default".
3. Next, tick the Social Networks, Promotions and Notifications boxes in the Categories section. This will allow you to intelligently sort emails into multiple folders and keep your inbox organised. If you wish, you can also activate Forums

4. Then go to the "Labels" tab and scroll down. If you find any unwanted labels at the bottom, hide them. After that, to create new labels on Gmail, click the

5. Give it a name, for example "Work". From now on,you can move all work-related e-mails under the heading

"You don't need to select anything. You don't need to select anything in the Nested drop-down menu

6. To identify an e-mail, simply click on the "arrow" button at the top and select the appropriate heading

7. To quickly find an email with the wording "Work", you can scroll down the list just below "Inbox" and click on "More". You'll find the "Work" label there. You can also move a label to the top of the Label settings page by hiding or showing it.

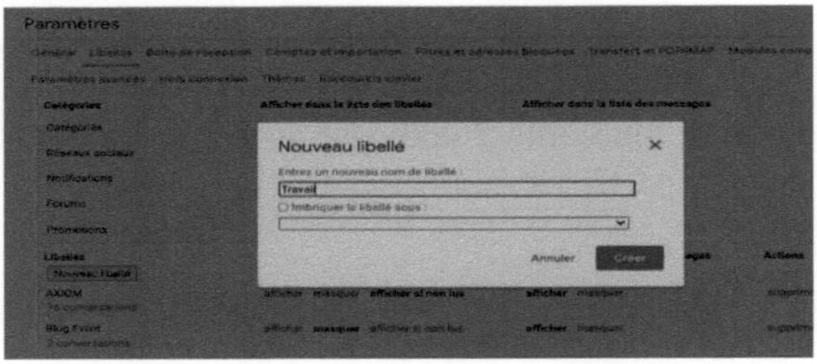

II.8. PERSONALISE YOUR EMAIL ACCOUNT

You can personalise the appearance of your mailbox by changing the background and colour, adding a signature to your e-mails or creating reply templates. This also makes it easier to organise your e-mails and save time. Don't forget to clean regularly your mailbox to at optimise how it works.

Change the look of your mailbox on Gmail

Follow these instructions:

1. Click on the cogwheel at the top right of the main window.

2. In the drop-down menu, click on "**Theme**" "**Show all**".

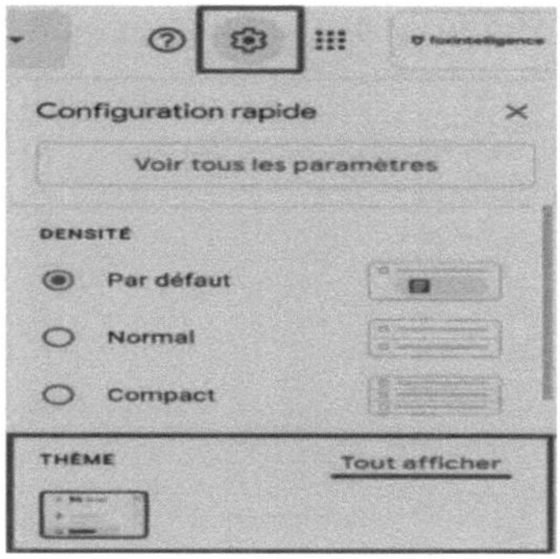

3. Scroll through the images and choose the one you like.

4. For obtain a choice more choice, click on Other images.

5. If you want to use an image on your hard drive, simply click on My Photos in the bottom left-hand corner (see screenshot above).
6. The grey icons at the bottom of the Choose a theme window allow you to customise the background colour for emails, add a vignetting effect or apply a background to the chosen image.

Change the look of your Hotmail mailbox

On **Hotmail** or Outlook, you can sort your e-mails into

files.

1. At the top of the email list, select Filter, then Sort by.

2. Choose the type of sort from the options available

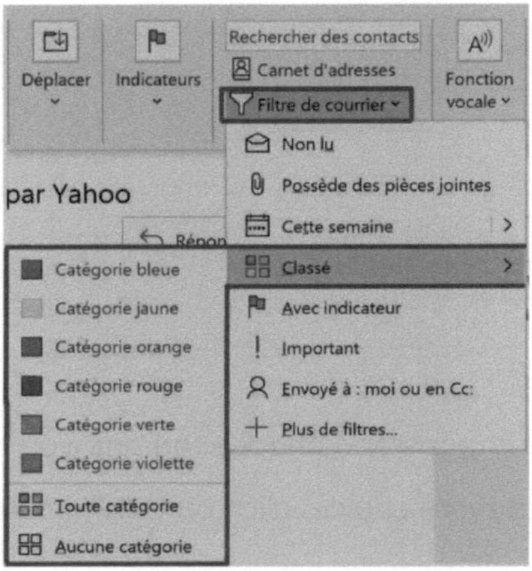

3. To sort your e-mails by conversation, in Settings, then Quick settings, select Most recent messages first or Most recent messages last.

Add a signature to your e-mails

To avoid typing your personal details all the time, use the automatic **signature**. This is a short personalised text at the end of each email. It's like a business card on the Web. It contains information about the sender: surname, first name, job title, company name and logo, telephone number, postal and e-mail address.

It can also contain the address of the company's website and/or blog, and icons linking to your social networking profiles. You can also insert an image or a hypertext link to your latest article.

Fill in your personal details

To add **personal information** to the emails you send, proceed as follows:

On Outlook :

1. Click on the cogwheel at the top right of the screen, then on **All settings.**
2. Click on **Mail**, then **Compose and reply**
3. In the editor, choose from 3 modes: Rich Text, HTML, Plain Text

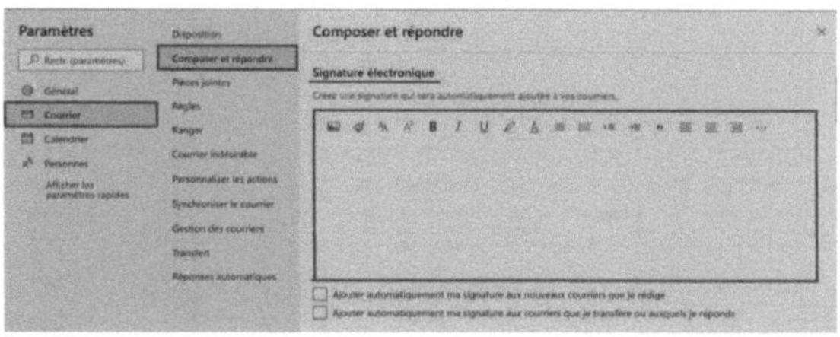

On **Gmail** :

1. Click on the cogwheel at the top right of the screen, then on

Parameters.

2. Click on **All settings**

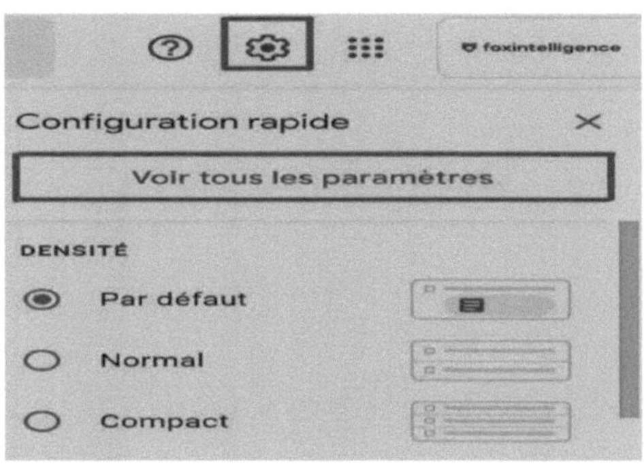

3. On the **General** tab, scroll to the **Signature** field.

4. Click on **Create** and fill in the **Signature** field in the text box with the required information

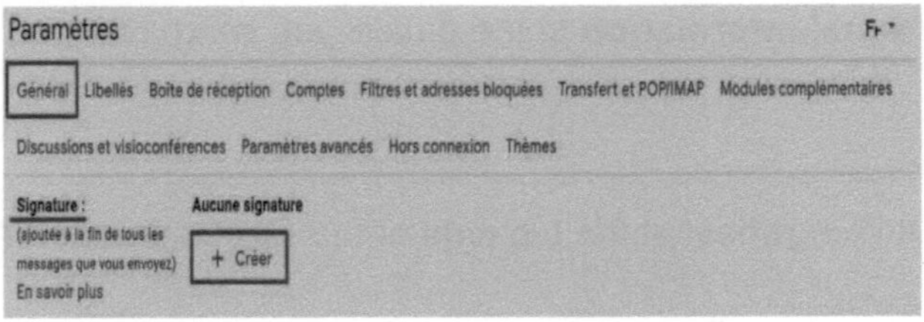

CHAPTER III
BURNING DATA ON CD

III.1.DEFINITION OF BURNING

Burning" is the common name for copying music, images and videos from a PC onto a blank CD or DVD. Conversely, 'ripping' involves copying music, images and videos from a CD or DVD to a PC[3] .

III.2.LAYOUT PRACTICE (Reader of player, Softwar specific,.)

Words to know :

CD, DVD

Both terms refer to physical media. The technical specifications for the CD were defined by Philips and Sony, initially as a music medium, with a recording capacity of 74 minutes or 650 MB of data. These specifications specify that the data is recorded on the medium in the form of a spiral 1.6 to 2.2 microns wide. The DVD is an evolution of the CD. It comes in four versions: the single-sided, single-layer DVD-5, which can store 4.7 GB of data; double-sided DVD-9 (8.5 GB); double-sided DVD-10 (9.4 GB) and double-sided double-layer DVD-18 (17 GB).CD-R, CD-RW, DVD-R, DVD-RW, DVD+R, DVD+RWAll these names correspond to recordable discs (by burning). The CD-R can be recorded only once, while the CD-RW can be re-recorded 1,000 times in theory, and 200 to 300 times in practice. For DVDs, a distinction is made between DVD and DVD+, which correspond to two different data recording techniques. DVD±Rs can be recorded once, while DVD±RWs can be re-recorded 1,000 times in theory, and 100 times in practice.

ISO 9660, Joliet, UDF

The Iso 9660 standard defines the structure of the data CD file system. Defined in 1988, it has evolved three times. Initially, it allowed only 8-letter file names with a 3-letter extension. It now allows 32 characters i n file names, with longer names being truncated. The Joliet standard, defined by Microsoft, is an extension of ISO 9660: it allows up to 64 characters and takes accented characters into account, but it is not accepted by all hardware, particularly home players. UDF (Universal Disk Format) was developed to replace Iso 9660: it allows data to be written to the disk on the fly.

VCD, SVCD

The VCD format allows videos in MPeg1 format to be stored on a CD, with 352 x 288 pixels and a maximum bit rate of 1.5 Mbit/s. The SVCD format is an evolution of the VCD: it is based on the MPeg2 format, and offers a definition of 480 x 576 pixels at a maximum bit rate of 2.5 Mbit/s. SVCD was launched in China in 1998 as an alternative to DVD-video.

Buffer memory, Burnproof

When writing a CD, the laser engraving process must not be interrupted, otherwise the disc will become unreadable. This means that data must be sent regularly and continuously from the disc controller to the recorder, which in practice is impossible. The recorders have therefore been fitted with a buffer memory to absorb any variations in the flow of data. This system is effective for low-speed burning, but insufficient for speeds above 12X. To overcome this limit, Sanyo has developed BurnProof technology. This monitors the state of the buffer memory and, in the event of a break in the data flow, pauses the laser on a predetermined area of the CD. This avoids wasting large numbers of CDs. Equivalent techniques are used today by all manufacturers, under various names (SafeBurn, SmartBurn, etc.).

MPEG, DIVX

The Motion Pictures Expert Group has defined several standards for digital video. MPeg1 allows video to be compressed to a definition of 352 x 288 dots at a maximum bit rate of 1.5 Mbit/s. MPeg2 allows a definition of 720 x 576 dots, with a maximum bit rate of 15 Mbit/s. DivX is based on the MPeg4 standard.allows different compression ratios, with the quality obtained depending on image definition and bit rate (generally between 800 and 1,500 kbit/s).

Overburning

A technique that allows more data to be burnt than the blank medium is designed to accept (a few dozen megabytes, or an extra 2 to 3 minutes on an audio CD, for example). This process is risky: the burnt disc may be unreadable or, worse still, the recorder may be damaged.

Which burner should you choose?

Internal or external?

If you want to use your recorder with several computers, choose an external model. Depending on the interface it is fitted with, you will plug it into a USB 2.0 or FireWire socket on your computer. Don't connect a USB recorder to a USB 1.0 socket; you'll be limited in burning speed and your discs could contain errors. If you don't need to move your writer, choose an internal model and connect it to your motherboard using an IDE ribbon cable.

CD or DVD?

CD burners only burn CDs, whereas DVD burners burn both DVDs and CDs. DVD burners are therefore more versatile, but they wear out more quickly when used with CDs.

Which formats?

All current recorders handle both CD-Rs and CD-RWs. But some DVD burners only recognise one recordable DVD format (DVD+ or DVD-). Forget them and choose a multi-format model that accepts both DVD+ and DVD-.

What speed?

Don't be fooled by burning speeds expressed in X numbers. All current CD burners record CD-Rs at 48X or more and CD-RWs at 32X, whereas it is neither useful nor advisable to burn them at more than 16X.

Similarly, for DVD burners, a speed of 2X is preferable to guarantee good quality burns. Keep an eye on the amount of buffer memory (preferably 2 MB) and the presence of a BurnProof device.

Essential software
Nero Express 6 (Nero OEM)
Price: supplied with the burner

Size: 100 Mb **Language:** French **Website:**

This light version of Nero 6 software is supplied with many burners. We have used it in the following pages for our step-by-step instructions. It is very complete, allowing you to create data CDs as well as audio CDs and DVDs, and to makeslideshows or simple video compilations. Unfortunately, it is not available as a trial version. If you don't have it, you can download a trial version of Nero 6, which has a very similar interface.

Easy CD-DA Extractor 7
Price: 30 euros **Size:** 5 Mb **Language:** English **Website:**
www.poikosoft.com
This software specialises in processing audio CDs. It can easily extract tracks and convert them to Wave, MP3, WMA or Ogg. It accepts CDs with the anti-piracy protection used by some record companies. Easy CD-DA Extractor 7 can also convert audio files from one format to another and burn audio CDs directly. Its strong point: speed.

CD & DVD Picture Lab 2
Price: 50 euros **Size:** 75 Mb **Language:** French **Website:**
www.ulead.fr
A veritable toolbox for digital photographers, this software

Ulead lets you organise your photos, retouch them (anti-eyestrain special effects), print them (with contact sheets) and create slideshows. It offers 42 different transition effects between photos and automatically creates menus for VCDs and SVCDs. Ready-to-use templates mean you can create your first slideshow in just a few minutes. The only drawback is that it is very slow on older PCs.

DVD MovieFactory 3

Price: 80 euros **Size:** 100 Mb **Language:** French **Website:** www.ulead.fr

High-performance software for creating DVD-videos. It can import videos directly from a digital camcorder and from most formats. DVD MovieFactory 3 lets you easily edit videos (cut, crop, etc.) and optimise their compression to suit the recording medium. It manages VCD, SVCD and DVD formats and includes a simulator for viewing your DVD-video before burning it.

III.2. ENGRAVING PROCESS

What do you want to engrave?

It is of the first question à to ask yourself since there exist differences between a data DVD and a so-called "readable" DVD.

Data DVDs can only be read by a computer.

Here, the burning process is the same as for a USB stick: simply add the files from your computer to the CD or DVD, then choose the burning software. The data burned in this way can be read from another computer but not erased (except in the case of a rewritable CD).

DVDs that can be read can be read from another medium: Video DVDs can be read from a DVD player.

In the case of a playable CD or DVD, the information is recorded in the form of an audio or video "stream" that can be decoded by a DVD player. A video DVD must be decoded and can only contain video files, unlike a data DVD, which can contain any type of file (document, photo, video, music, etc.).

2. Burning a data CD or DVD under Windows 10: methods.

Method 1: Using Windows 10's built-in burning function

- Insert a blank CD or DVD into the CD/DVD burner

• Open Windows **File Explorer**

• Select all the files you want from their location
• Right-click then **Send** to and choose the CD to be burned• A **Burn a disc** window appears
• Enter a disk name

• Select **With a CD/DVD drive**, then click **Next**.

files are now copied. Your CD/DVD drive opens:

• Copy the files to the drive

• Click on **Drive tools**
• Click on **Finish burning**

Method 2: With Windows 10 Media Player

• Insert a blank CD or DVD

• Open **Windows Media Player**

• Click on **Burn** (top right)

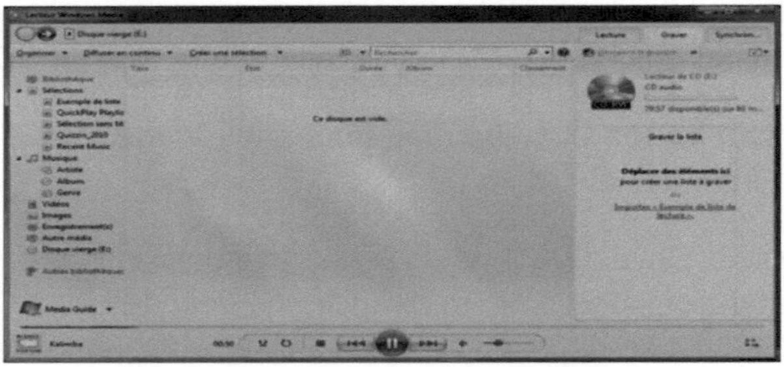

• Click on **Burning Options** and choose Data CD or DVD (for playback on PCs and certain players that support these formats) or Audio CD (to burn MP3, WMA or WAV files for playback on all CD players and car radios).
• Open **Windows File Explorer** and go to the location of your files

• Make sure you can see both the **File Explorer** and **Windows Media**

Player windows simultaneously

- Select your files and drag them to the burn list

Windows Media Player

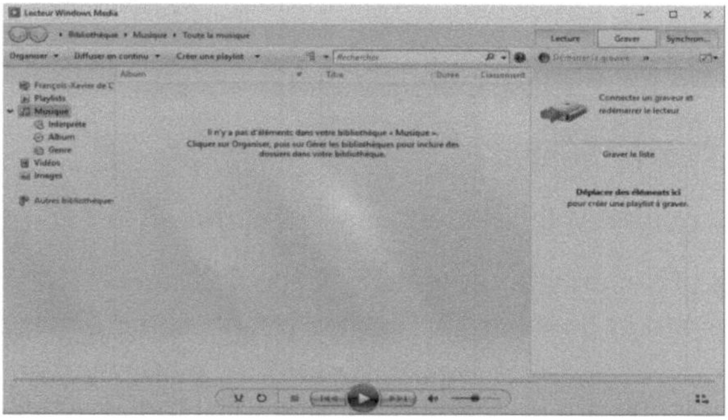

- Rearrange the order of your files if necessary
- Finally, click on **Start burning**

Windows will burn your CD or DVD and you will see a progress bar appear until the process is complete.

III.3. SECURITY CONDITIONS FOR STORAGE MEDIA

A well-organised and coherent storage and security system is essential to meet the short-term data storage needs of research projects. Securely stored data is much easier to consult, understand, discover and share with the scientific community and the general public. A data storage strategy, for both digital and non-digital materials, is essential for the long-term preservation of data. As all digital and physical storage media are inherently unreliable and will eventually become obsolete, a data storage strategy must be put in place before any project begins.We're always happy to answer your questions and help you further. We look forward to hearing from you.

Short-term data storage

Short-term data storage needs have elements that are both similar and distinct from long-term retention requirements.

Things to bear in mind when planning data storage :

- How much data is created?
- How many people will have access to the data?
- What level of security is required?
- The data private or confidential sont-ellesencrypted or password-protected?
- Is anti-virus software installed on your computer(s
- +How often is data backed up?
- Where can I find the backup files?
- How long are backups kept?
- Is the location secure?
- What are the costs associated with short-term storage?
- Are the master files stored in another secure location?
- +How long will the data be kept?

Storage media

The accessibility of any data depends on the quality of the storage media on which it is stored and the availability of appropriate data reading equipment.If you choose optical media (CDs, DVDs) or magnetic media (hard disks) for storage, be aware that both are sensitive and vulnerable to mishandling, changes in temperature and relative humidity, as well as air quality and lighting conditions.The speed of technological progress has a direct impact on the rate at which media and equipment become obsolete.For these reasons, data files should be copied and backed up (i.e. migrated) onto new media every two to five years. The quality and readability of all media should be checked regularly. See below for more details on file migration.

Data loss can be caused by :

- Hardware failure
- Software or support failure
- Virus infection or malicious hacking
- Power failure
- Human error, such as the modification or deletion of files or the loss of a storage device
- A natural disaster, such as a flood or fire

If you use cloud storage facilities, take into account where the data is housed and the jurisdiction over it. There are other factors to consider:

- Long-term costs
- The longevity of the service provider
- Data security and confidentiality
- The content of intellectual property and data protection agreements

CHAPTER IV
DATA SORTING IV.1.DEFINITION

Sorting data involves selecting a data area and then sorting its rows (or columns) according to one or more criteria - in ascending or descending order depending on the value of one or more columns (or rows, if you are sorting columns of data).

IV.2. ROLES

Data sorting has multiple roles, including :

1. Monitoring errors

It is necessary to have a record of the trends from which most of your errors originate. This will make it much easier to identify and correct incorrect or corrupted data. Records are particularly important if you are integrating other solutions with your fleet management software, so that your errors do not impede the work of other departments.

2. Standardise your process

Standardising the entry point reduces the risk of duplication.

3. Validate the accuracy of the data

Once you have cleaned up your existing database, validate the accuracy of your data. Search and Invest in tools that allow you to clean up your data in real time. Some tools even use AI or machine learning to better test accuracy.

4. Sort duplicate data

Identifying duplicates saves time when analysing data. Duplicate data can be avoided by researching and investing in various data cleansing tools that can analyse raw data en masse and automate the process for you.

5. Analysing your data

Once the data has been standardised, validated and sorted for duplicates, use third-party sources to add it. Reliable third-party sources can capture information directly from proprietary sites, then clean and compile the data to provide more comprehensive information for business intelligence and analysis. Finally, it is necessary to regularly monitor and examine the data in order to detect inconsistencies.

IV.3. DATA SORTING USING SIMPLE METHODS

Sorting is one of the most common data management tools. In Excel, you can sort your table into one or more columns, in ascending or descending order, or perform a custom sort.

Sort the table

1. Select a cell in the data.

2. Select **Home** > **Sort and filter**.

Or select **Data** > **Sort**.

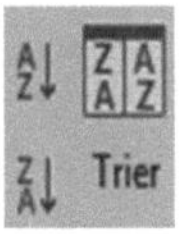

3. Select an option :

► **Sort from A to Z**: sorts the selected column in ascending order.

► **Sort from Z to A**: sorts the selected column in descending order.

► **Tripersonalized**: sorts the data by several columns, using different sorting criteria.

Here's how to create a custom sort:

1. Select **Custom sort**.
2. Select **Add a level**.

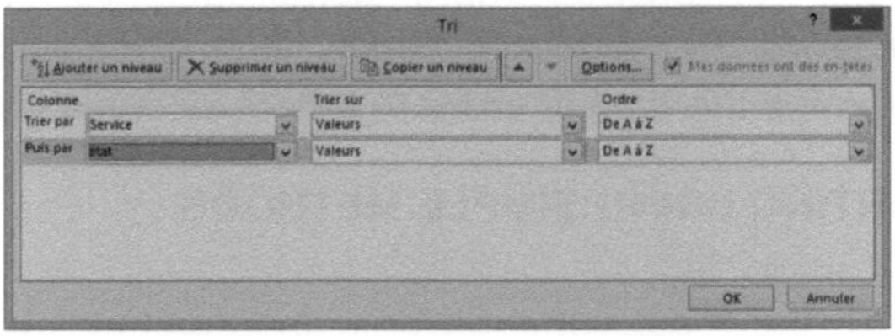

3. For **Column**, in the drop-down list, select the first column to be used for sorting (**Sort by**), then the second (**Then by**). For example, the Department column for **Sort by**, and the Status column for **Then by**.
4. To **Sort on**, select **Values**.
5. For **Order**, select an option (for example, **A to Z**, **Smallest to Largest** or **Largest to Smallest**).
6. For each additional column you wish to use for sorting, repeat steps 2 to 5.

Note: To delete a level, select **Delete level.**

7. If your data includes a header line, activate the **My data has headers** checkbox.
8. Select **OK**.

IV.4. APPLICATION OF SORTING TO ACCOUNTING DATA

The Sort temporary rows function

This tool can be used to quickly sort content according to the column from which the **Sort** function is given :

- Right-click on the header of the column to be sorted.
- Position yourself on the small arrow and select ascending or descending sorting criteria.

Benefits

- You can **sort the lines displayed,** in ascending or descending order, according to the column you want.
- Unlike Excel, **when you remove the sort from the display, the rows return to their original order** without the need to use the Undo command.

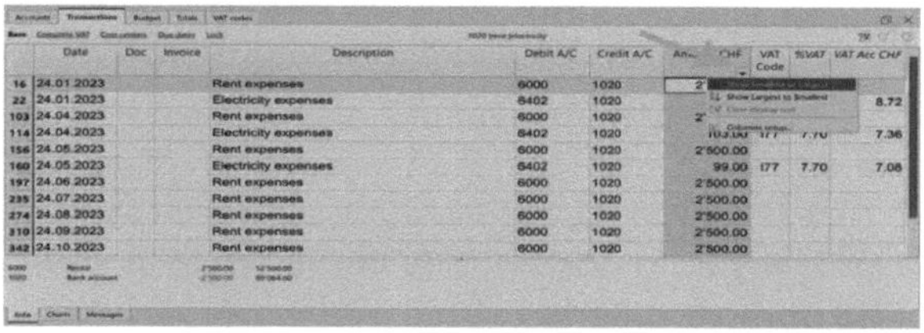

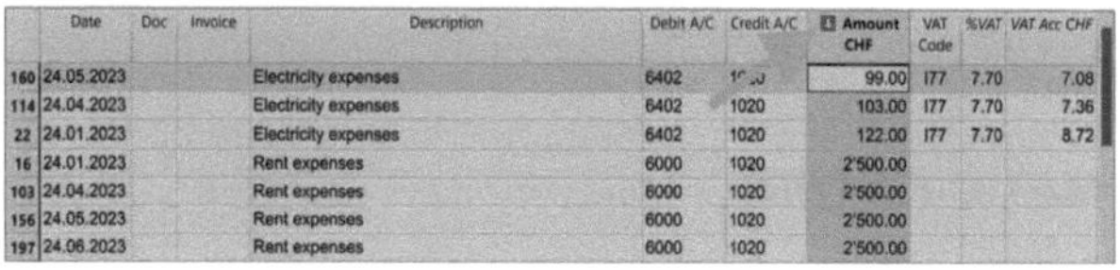

An arrow appears in the header of the column chosen to sort the data.

NB: The **Sort temporary rows** function is different from the

Sort rows (in the Data menu) :

- **Temporary line sort** is a temporary on-screen line sort designed to speed up the review and editing of previously entered data; you can easily remove the sort to return to the original line order. This function is only available with the Advanced plan.
- The Sort rows command (in the Data menu) permanently changes the order of the rows in the table and can only be undone using the **Undo** command. This command is available for all

CHAPTER V
DATA FILTERS

V.1.DEFINITION

Filtering data consists of selecting, using one or more criteria, the column values to be filtered, the rows to be displayed and those to be hidden[4] .

V.2. ROLE

The data filter allows you to display only certain data in your table, according to one or more criteria.

V.3. TYPES

V.3.1. AUTOMATIC FILTER

The automatic filter allows the user to display only those lines in the table that meet the criteria of their choice, temporarily masking the others. Once the required information has been obtained, the user removes the filter: the table reappears in its entirety.

Proceed as follows to apply an automatic filter:

1. Select the data to filter.
2. Click on **Data** > **Filter**.
3. Click on the arrow in the column header and decide whether you want to select specific values or perform a search.

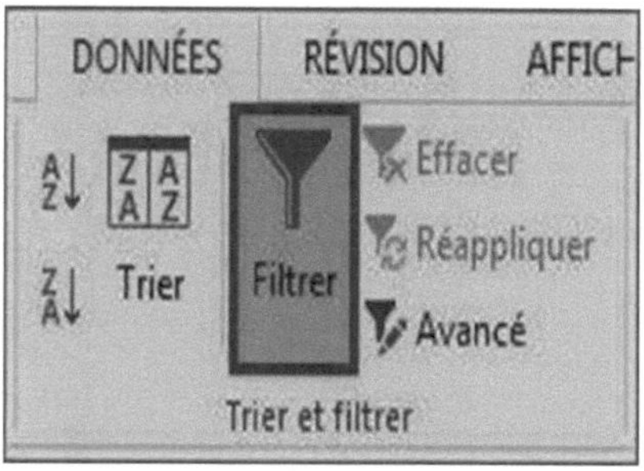

4. **Choose specific values:** Uncheck **(Select all)** to delete all the activated box fields, then activate the boxes corresponding to the specific values you want to display.

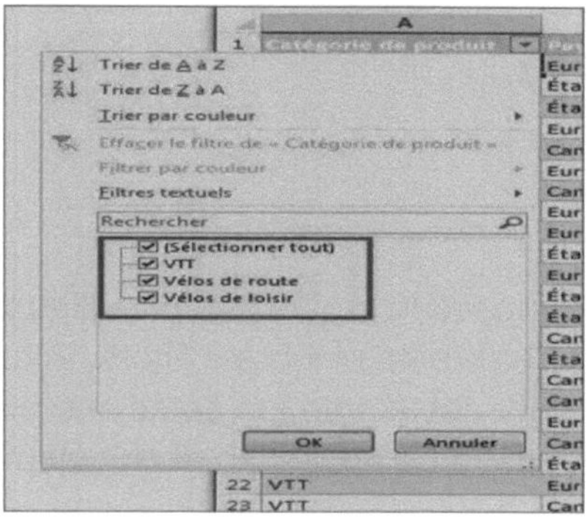

5. **Search for values:** In the **Search box**, type the text or numbers you are looking for.

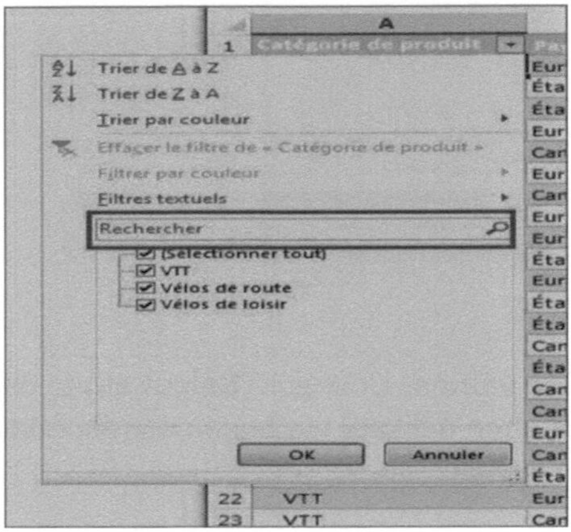

6. Click **OK** to apply the filter.

V.3.2. FILTER

Advanced filters can be used to create complex filters, with no limit on the number of criteria. To create elaborate filters, you need to copy the column headings from the table onto the same sheet or another sheet, and then write the criteria to be applied to each column.

EXAMPLES

Let's start with a simple case: filter the rows (records) where the **Location** column is equal to "Brussels".

In cell **B2**, just below the **Location** label, we enter the value "Brussels".

In the Sort and filter group on the **[Data]** tab, click **Advanced.** The **Advanced Filter** dialog box appears.

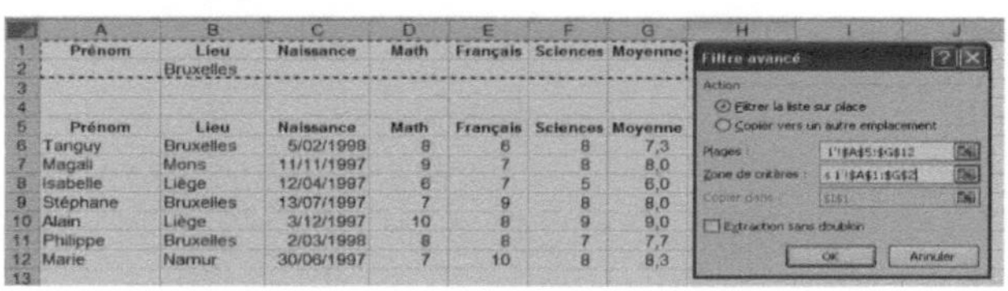

Let's analyse each option in this box.

- **Filter the list on the spot**: filter directly in the Excel cell area where the initial data is placed and which is declared by the **Ranges** option (in our example **A5:G12**).
- **Copy to another location**: creates the filtered list in another location defined by the **Copy to** option.
- **Ranges**: the area to be filtered.

- **Criteria area**: designates the range of cells where we have inserted our filter criteria (in our example **A2:G2**).
- **Copy to**: designates the cell or range of cells from which the filtered rows will be copied. This option is only available if **Copy to another location** is ticked.
- **Extraction without duplicates**: allows you to avoid displaying duplicate data, either with the filter in place, or by copying to another location.

We therefore opt for the in-place filter, taking the range as **A5:G12** and the criteria area as **A1:G2**. Confirm with **OK** and see the result.

	A	B	C	D	E	F	G
1	Prénom	Lieu	Naissance	Math	Français	Sciences	Moyenne
2		Bruxelles					
3							
4							
5	Prénom	Lieu	Naissance	Math	Français	Sciences	Moyenne
6	Tanguy	Bruxelles	5/02/1998	8	6	8	7,3
9	Stéphane	Bruxelles	13/07/1997	7	9	8	8,0
11	Philippe	Bruxelles	2/03/1998	8	8	7	7,7
13							

We can see that the filtered row numbers are blue and that rows 7, 8, 10 and 12 are hidden: this is because the value contained in these rows is different from the criterion chosen ("Brussels").

This result could, of course, have been obtained using a simple filter.

To display the data again, simply click on the **Clear** command, which is in the same group as the **Advanced filter** command.

Second example

Let's now filter out the records for which the location is "Brussels" AND whose date of birth is greater than or equal to 1er January 2008.
So let's add the value >=01/01/2008 to cell **C2**. Then run the same command, choosing the same options.

	A	B	C	D	E	F	G
1	Prénom	Lieu	Naissance	Math	Français	Sciences	Moyenne
2		Bruxelles	>=01/01/1998				
3							
4							
5	Prénom	Lieu	Naissance	Math	Français	Sciences	Moyenne
6	Tanguy	Bruxelles	5/02/1998	8	6	8	7,3
11	Philippe	Bruxelles	2/03/1998	8	8	7	7,7
13							

We can see that there are now only two recordings that meet these two criteria combined.

Third example

Then apply a filter by adding a criterion:(Location=Brussels and Date of birth>=01/01/1998) **OR** (Average>7.5).To obtain the desired result, we add the value **>7.5** to **G3** (**Average** column**)**.In the dialog box, change the criteria field toA1:G3.

	A	B	C	D	E	F	G
1	Prénom	Lieu	Naissance	Math	Français	Sciences	Moyenne
2		Bruxelles	>=01/01/1998				
3							>7,5
4							
5	Prénom	Lieu	Naissance	Math	Français	Sciences	Moyenne
6	Tanguy	Bruxelles	5/02/1998	8	6	8	7,3
7	Magali	Mons	11/11/1997	9	7	8	8,0
9	Stéphane	Bruxelles	13/07/1997	7	9	8	8,0
10	Alain	Liège	3/12/1997	10	8	9	9,0
11	Philippe	Bruxelles	2/03/1998	8	8	7	7,7
12	Marie	Namur	30/06/1997	7	10	8	8,3

In conclusion, we can see that placing criteria on the same line is equivalent to the **AND** function; however, if we use several lines, this is equivalent to the **OR** function.

V.4. FILTER APPLICATIONS ON ACCOUNTING DATA

On Indy, use the filter to navigate from month to month, year to year, make only one account visible and much more...

The filter function is available to the right of the search bar in the **Transactions** tab.

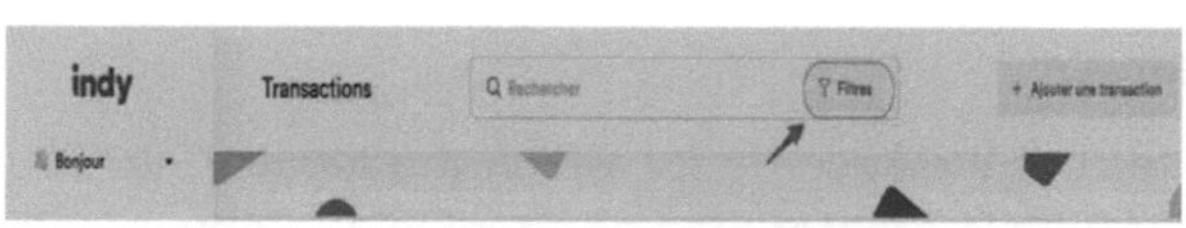

Date range

Navigate from month to month

Indy limits the display to 400 transactions in order to maintain optimum performance (and to avoid you having to download an endless list of transactions).
By clicking on **Start - End** under **Range of dates**, a calendar will open, allowing you to choose the exercise you wish to highlight.

Simply click on the exercise you are looking for to display the selection.

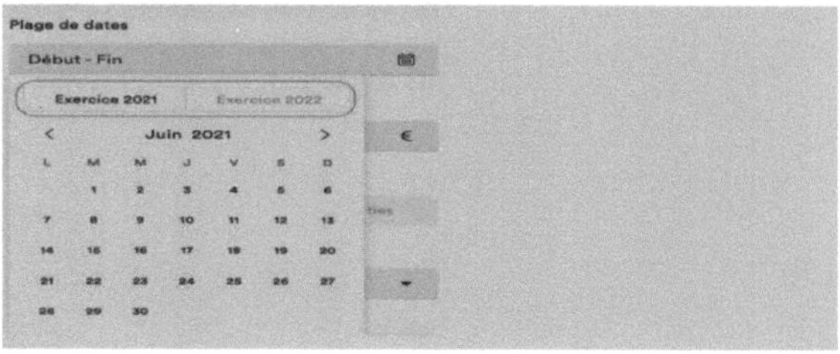

Navigate from month to month

Still by clicking on **Range of dates**, you can choose the month you want by clicking on the 1st and last day of the month in question.

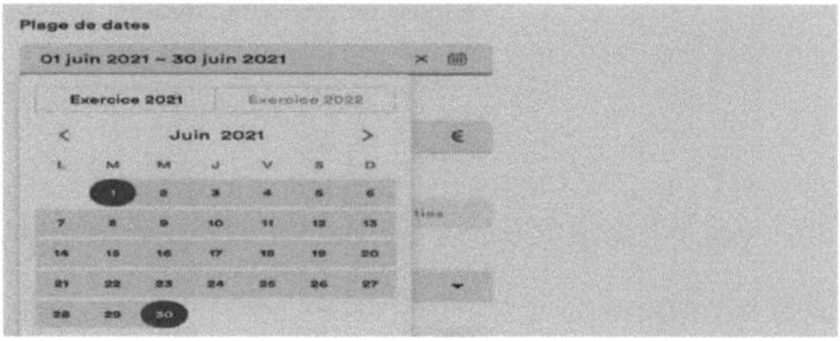

Select a period

You can further refine your search by highlighting the desired you want.
To do this, simply click on the first day of the period, then the last.
This also applies to one search per day.

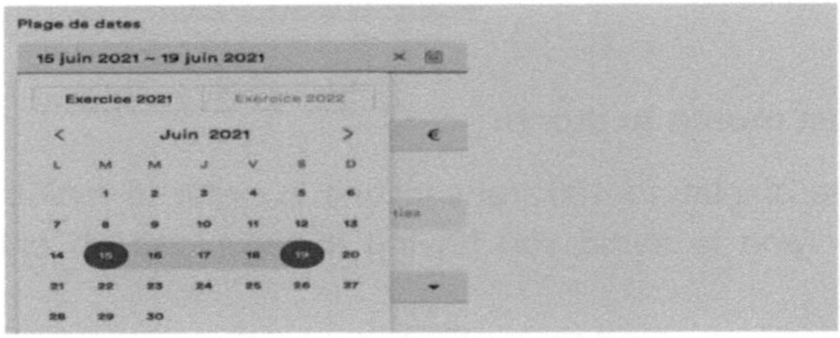

Range of uprights

You can use this filter to find a transaction (or several!) by amount.

Inputs / outputs

This function allows you to filter your transactions by **Cash In** or **Cash Out**.

Categories

Here you can filter your transactions by accounting category.

Categories can be combined.

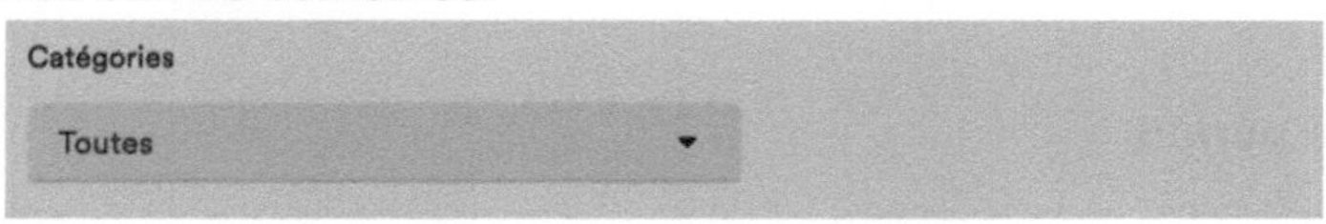

Supporting documents

By default set to All, you can choose to display transactions to which a receipt has been linked or all those that do not.

VAT to be defined

This filter will allow you to display transactions to which no VAT rate has been assigned, so that you can find them more easily.

Type of transaction

From **Transaction type**, you can choose to display :

- **The** bank account of your choice (useful if you have more than one)7)
- **Deferred debit card account**
- **The till**: all your cash movements when you clicked on **+ Add transaction ➤ Cash receipt/spending**
- **Expense reports**: all the transactions you have entered manually by clicking on **+ Add a transaction ➤ Expense report**
- **Receipts on personal account**: all transactions that you have entered manually by clicking on **+ Add a transaction ➤ Receipts on personal account**
- **Miscellaneous operations**: all the entries generated automatically by Indy, such as depreciation, accruals, mileage allowances, etc.

Reset

You can click **Reset** at any time to cancel all the filters you have selected.

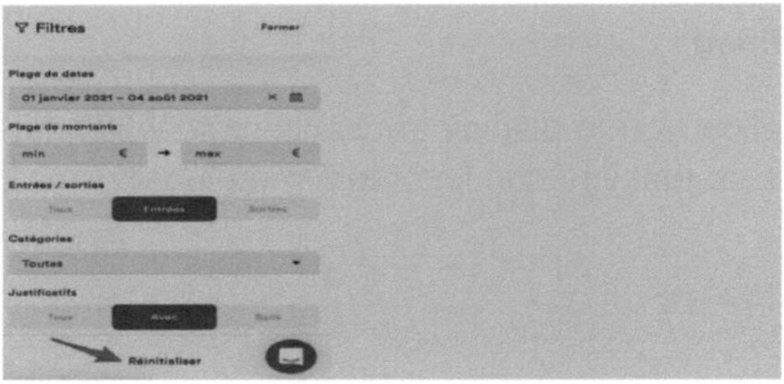

Filter line function

The **Filter rows** function lets you quickly filter table rows by extracting what you are looking for. **It saves you a considerable amount of time**, because :

- You can find the entries you want in a matter of seconds. • You can modify the filtered entries directly.
- The Temporary Filter is present in all the tables in the file (Accounts, Transactions, etc.) and to use it, all you have to do is type some keywords in the filter box
- You can easily remove the filter to return to the original order of the lines.

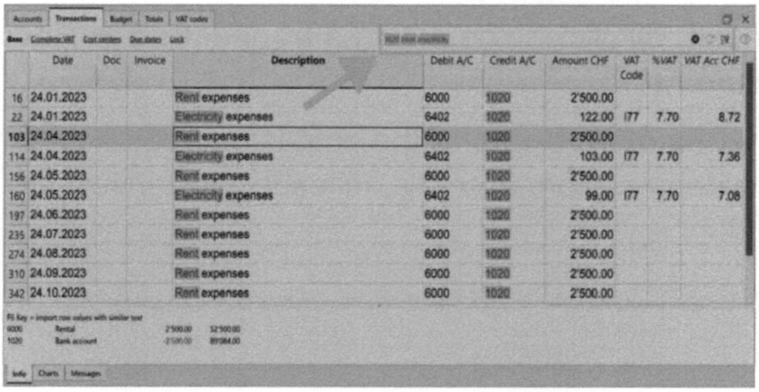

CHAPTER VI
GRAPHICS

VI.1. DEFINITION

It is a representation of the data in a form that can behelp you and your audience understand the relationships between them[5]

VI.2. ROLES

1. Clearly represent lists of abstract numbers ;

2. You can compare your data in the form of bars, circles and lines;
3. Explaining trends and visualising facts;

4. Frequent processing of large volumes of data.

VI.3. ENTER DATA

In the worksheet containing the data for your graph, in the cells directly next to or below your existing source data for the graph, enter the new series of data you want to add.In this example, we have a graph displaying quarterly sales data for 2013 and 2014, and we've just added a new series of data to the 2015 spreadsheet. Note that the chart does not yet display the 2015 data series.

1. Click anywhere on the graph.

The source data currently displayed is selected in the worksheet, using the reizing handles.You will notice that the 2015 data series is not selected.

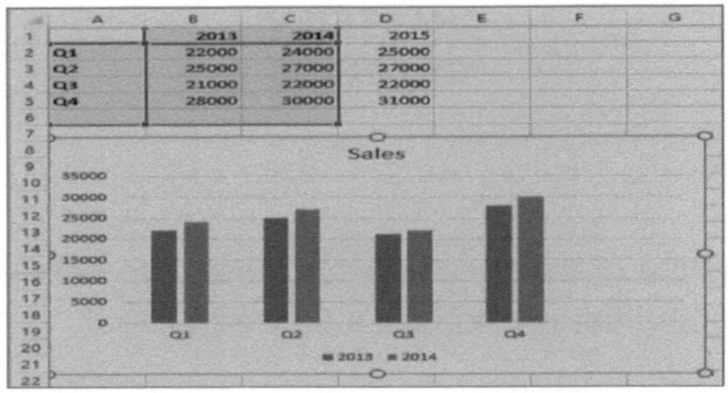

2. In the sheet ofworksheet, go to drag the handles to include the new data.

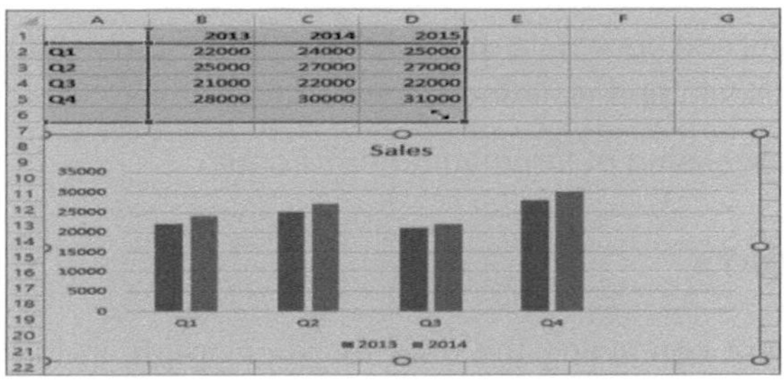

The graph is updated automatically, displaying the new series of data you have added.

VI.4. CONSTRUCTION OF GRAPHICS

The Graph Builder allows you to create graphs from predefined graphs in the gallery or from specific components (for example, axes and bars). To create a chart, drag basic elements or charts from the gallery and drop them onto the **canvas**, which is the area to the right of the Variables list in the Chart Generator dialog box.

VI.4.1. HISTOGRAMS

A histogram is a graphical representation of data. It shows the distribution of data by displaying the number of data points that fall within a certain range of values[6] .

To create a histogram :

1. Enter data in a spreadsheet.
2. Select the data.
3. In the **Insert** tab, select **Insert a column or bar chart**, then choose a histogram option.

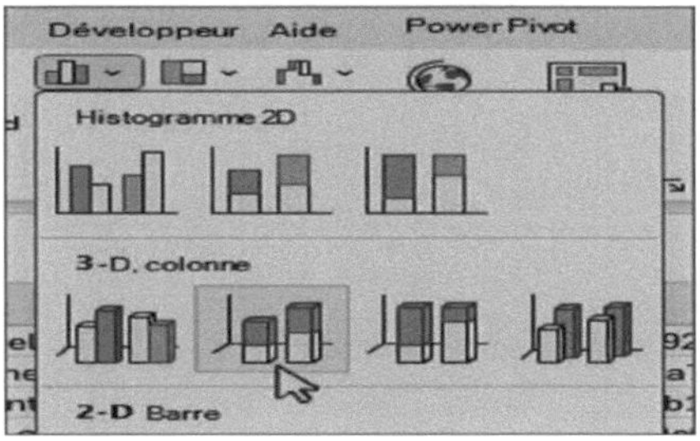

You can format the graph if you wish:

Note: Make sure you select the graphic before applying aformatting option.

- To apply a different chart layout, in the **Chart creation** tab, select **Chart layout**, then choose a layout.
- To apply a different chart style, in the **Chart creation** tab, select **Chart styles** and then choose a style.
- To apply a different shape style, in the **Format** tab, select Shape **styles**, then choose a style.

Note: Chart styles and shape styles are two different things. A shape style is a formatting option that applies to the border of the graph only, whereas a graph style is a formatting option that applies to the whole graph.

- To apply different shape effects, in the **Format** tab, select Shape **effects**, then choose an option such as **Bevel** or **Light**, then a sub-option.
- To apply a theme, on the **Page Setup** tab, select

Themes, then choose a theme.

- To apply a formatting option to a specific component of a chart (for example, Vertical Axis (value),Horizontal Axis (category),Chart Area, etc.), on the **Format** tab, select a component from the **Chart Elements** drop-down list box, select Format of **selection**, and then make the necessary changes. Repeat the step for each component you wish to modify.

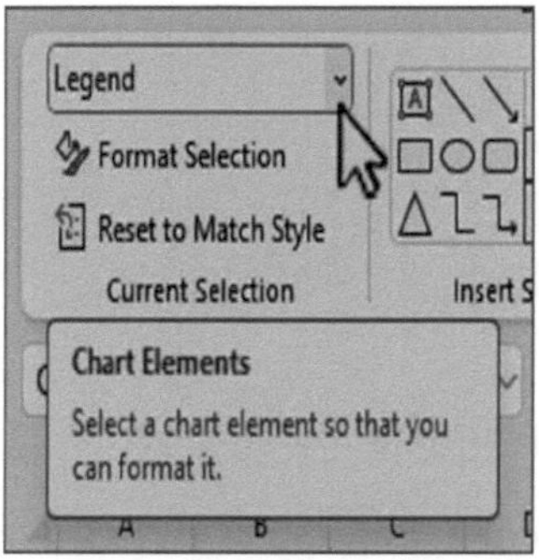

Note: If you are used to working with graphs, you can also select and right-click on a specific area of the graph, then select a formatting option.

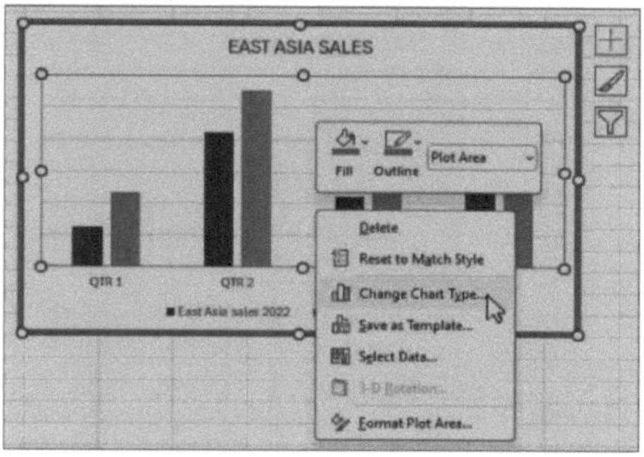

VI.4.2. DIAGRAMS AT STICKS

The **bar chart**, also known as the frequency chart, is a graphical representation of a statistical series of discrete quantitative variables. For each value, a vertical segment or rectangle is associated, the height of which is proportional to the known value (number or frequency). It is used to highlight the observed distribution of modalities and to visualise the dispersion of observations.

VI.4.3. SECTOR

A pie chart (also known as a pie graph or pie chart) is a circular statistical graph, divided into parts, and illustrating a numerical proportion. In a pie chart, the arc length of each share, and therefore its central angle and area, are proportional to the quantity it represents. A pie chart can only display one series of data. Excel uses the identifier of this series as the chart title (e.g. "Flowers") and displays the values of this series in proportional parts on the pie chart. This type of The graph is well suited to showing the distribution of a value within a dimension, such as Sales per representative.

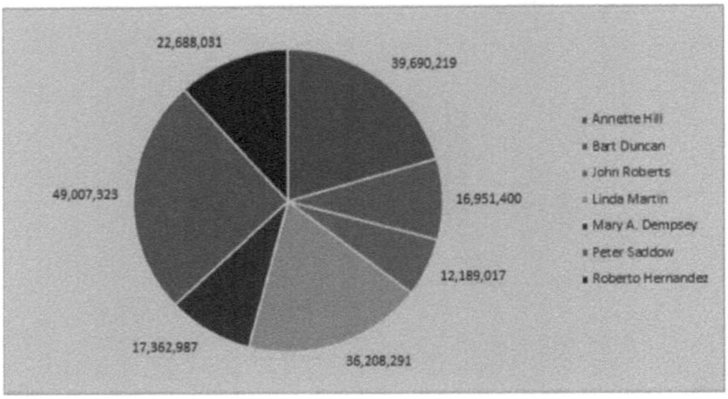

VI.4.4. CURVES

A line graph is a basic type of graph, frequently used to represent information in the form of a set of data points, called "markers", connected by straight line segments. A line graph is often used to visualise the evolution of certain data over a period of time, with the curve most often following a chronological order. This type of graph is recommended for comparing the evolution of several values, for example the Quantities available by product category over time.

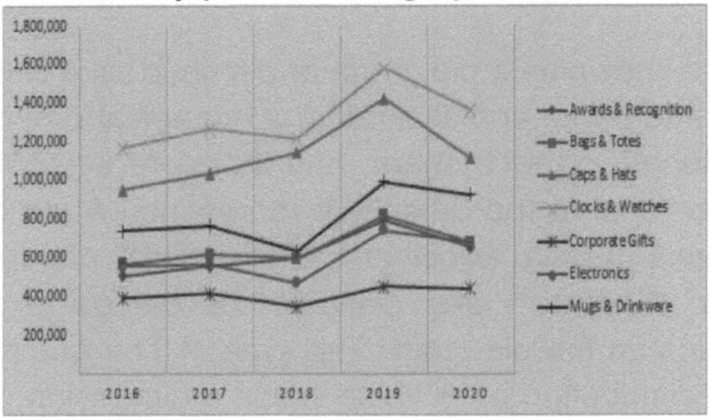

VI.4.5. AIRE

3D area graphics

3D area charts display the evolution of values over a period or other categorical data, and use three editable axes (horizontal, vertical and depth). This type of chart is recommended for comparing the distribution of a value within a category and its chronological evolution, such as the Evolution of sales by region.

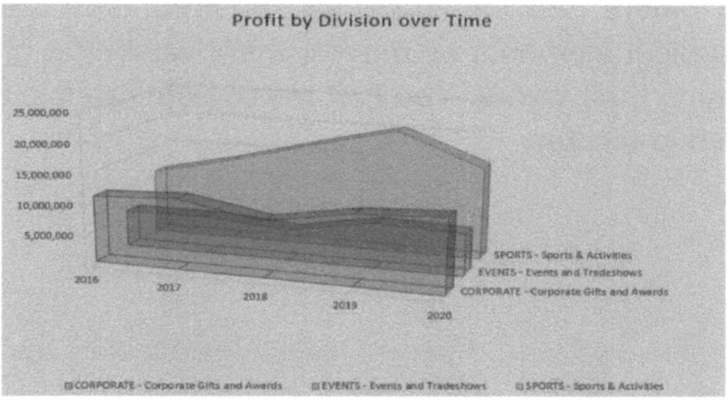

Stacked area graph

A stacked area graph shows the evolution of the contribution of each value over a given period or other categorical data. It is advisable to explain the stacked chart to users so that they can understand the values presented. A 3D stacked area chart is presented in the same way, but uses a 3D perspective and does not have a third axis. This type of graph is relevant for showing how different variables contribute to the total value over time.

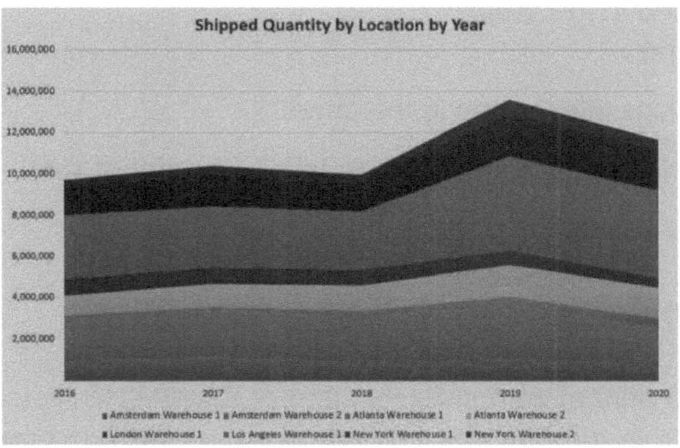

VI.5. DISPLAYING GRAPHS IN A SPREADSHEET

A graphic has many elements. Some of these elements appear by default, while others can be added as required. You can modify the display of graphical elements by moving them within the graph, resizing them or changing their layout. You can also delete graphic elements that you do not wish to display.

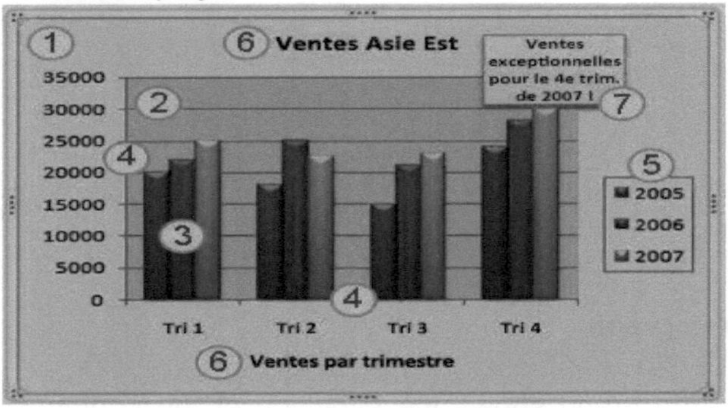

1. graph area of the chart.

2. plot area.

3. data points of the data series plotted in the graph.

4. horizontal axis (abscissa) and vertical axis (ordinate) along which the data are plotted in the graph.

5. graph legend.

6. Chart and axis title for use in the chart.

7. a data label used to identify the details of a point of sale.

data in a data series.

VI.6. PRINTING

If you need to print a chart in Excel 2013 or Excel 2016, you can use the **Print** option from the **File** tab. You can use the **Settings** menu to specify exactly what you want to print from your workbook.

1. Click on the graph in your workbook.

2. Click on **File** > **Print**.

NB: You can also use the keyboard shortcut Ctrl + P to open the **Print** option.

3. Click on the menu drop-down menu **Printer**, then selec the printer you want to use.

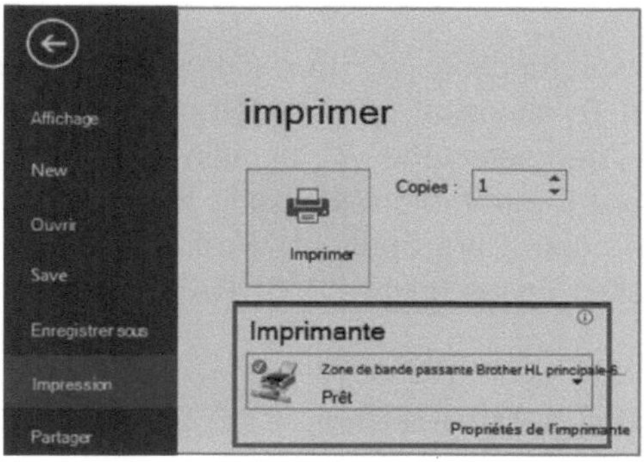

4. Click on **Print**.

NB: You can use the **Settings** option to identify the specific item you wish to print. Click on the **Settings** drop-down menu, then click on **Print Selected Graph** to print just the graph, or click on **Print Entire Workbook** to print the entire workbook.

CHAPTER VII

FINANCIAL FUNCTIONS EXCEL

VII.1. CALCULATION OF EARNED VALUE USING THE COMPOUND INTEREST FORMULA

The **sum of the capital invested and the interest it has earned over the term of the investment** is known as the earned value of a capital[7] .

The Excel financial function VC (for Cumulative Value) makes this calculation easier. To access it, start by left-clicking on the fx icon in the standard toolbar. Then select the VC function from the Finance functions category. There are 5 parameters for using this function. The first 3 are mandatory and the last 2 are optional. We'll look at their use later. The VC function is called up as follows: VC (RATE; NPM; VPM; VA; Type) where

RATES	Periodic rate (i)
VPM	Set to 0 or leave blank
NPM	Number of periods (n)
VA	Present value (PV)
Type	Optional(leaveempty or put 0)

An example. What is the value acquired by \$100 in 4 years at a rate of 8% compounded half-yearly?

Solution: Simply use the function VC (4%; 8; 0; 100; 0) and Excel will give a value of -\$136.86. The negative sign is explained by the fact that the money will "travel" in the opposite direction. You need to deposit \$100 toto withdraw \$136.86. If you want the final answer to be positive, enter : VC (4%; 8; 0; -100; 0).

VII.2. PRESENT VALUE CALCULATIONS USING THE COMPOUND INTEREST FORMULA

The Excel VA financial function makes it easier to perform this calculation. To access it, start by left-clicking on the fx icon in the standard toolbar. Then select the VA function from the Finance functions category. There are 5 parameters for using this function. The first 3 are mandatory and the last 2 are optional. We'll look at their use later. Function VA is called up as follows: VA (RATE; NPM; VPM; VC; Type) where

RATES	Periodic rate (i)
NPM	Number of periods (n)
VPM	Set to 0 or leave blank
VC	Earned value (EV)
Type	Optional(leave empty or put 0)

Example: We want to have $8,000 in capital in 15 years by depositing a certain amount of money today in a financial institution that pays interest at an annual rate of 10%. How much money should be deposited?
Solution: Simply use the Excel function VA(10%; 15; 0; 8000; 0) and Excel will give the value of -1915.14. Once again, the answer is negative because the money is travelling in the opposite direction. To be able to withdraw $8000 in 15 years' time, you need to start by depositing $1915.14 today. If we wants the final answer to be positive, enter : VC (10%; 1; 0 ;-8000;0

VII.3. CALCULATION OF THE INTEREST RATE

Let's say a bank advertises that if you deposit $500 each month for 12 years, you will have $100,000 at the end of the period.
What is the interest rate paid by the bank? To answer this question, use the RATE function, which returns the interest rate per annuity period.
RATE (nper; pmt; pv; fv; type; guess) ;

NPER : The total number of payment periods in an annuity ;

PMT: The payment made each period, which is a constant value ;
PV: Present value. This is the amount that a series of payments future is worth ;

FV: Future value. This is the amount you want after the last payment ;

TYPE: A number indicating when payments are due. 0 or omitted indicates the end of the period and 1 indicates the start of the period; Assumption: an assumption of the interest rate. If omitted, Excel uses 10%.

To calculate the interest rate :

1. In cell B1, enter the number of periods in years.
2. In cell B2, enter the monthly amount to be deposited.
3. In cell B3, enter the final value announced by the bank.
4. In cell B5, type the following formula: =RATES(B1*12; -B2; 0; B3; 0)*12.
5. Press <Enter>.

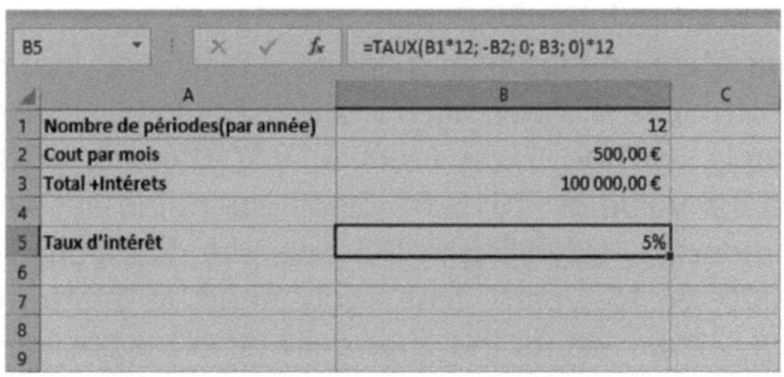

B5 | =TAUX(B1*12; -B2; 0; B3; 0)*12

	A	B	C
1	Nombre de périodes(par année)	12	
2	Cout par mois	500,00 €	
3	Total +Intérets	100 000,00 €	
4			
5	Taux d'intérêt	5%	
6			
7			
8			
9			

VII.4. CALCULATING THE EARNED VALUE OF A SUITE OF EQUAL PAYMENTS

The Excel function VA (for Valeur Actuelle) is used to perform this calculation. There are 5 parameters for using this formula. The first 3 are mandatory and the last 2 are optional. The VA function i s called as follows:VA (RATE; NPM; VPM; VC; Type)

RATES	Periodic rate (i)
NPM	Number of payments (n)
VPM	Value of each payment (PMT)
VC	Optional (leave blank or set to 0)
Type	0 if end of period annuity; 1 if start of period annuityperiod

Note: The result will have the opposite sign to VPM.

E.g.: How much debt must be repaid in 12 monthly instalments of $250 at the end of each period, at an interest rate of 2% per month?
Solution: This amount corresponds to the present value of the 12 payments of $250.
Using the function VC (2%; 12; -250; 0;0), we obtain PV = $2,643.84

VII.5. CALCULATION OF THE NUMBER OF PAYMENTS IN THE CASE OF A ENNUITE

The NPM function can be used to find n in the formulae: FV=PMT.$s_{\overline{n}/i}$ or FV=PMT. $a_{\overline{n}/i}$The NPM function is called up as follows

as follows:

NPM (RATE, VPM, VA, VC, Type)

RATES	Periodic rate (i)
VA	Present value of payments (PV)
Type	0 if annuity at end of period; 1 if annuity at beginning of period
VPM	Value of payments (PMT)
VC	Earned value of payments (EVA)

Example: How many end-of-month payments of $200 do you have to make to pay off a $5,000 debt today if the interest rate is 9%, compounded monthly, and the first payment is made one month after the loan.

Solution: With NPM (0.75%; -200; 5000; 0; 0), we find n =27.789 In other words, there are 27 monthly repayments of $200 and a 28ème of a value of less than $200 that could take place at the end of the 28ème month.

VII.6. CALCULATION OF THE PRICE OF A BOND AT A DATE OF COUPON

This calculation can be performed using the Excel VA function. Calling theThe VA function is then calculated as follows: VA (RATE; NPM; VPM; VC; Type)

RATE S	Desired periodic rate of return or market rate (i)
VPM	Value of each coupon (C)
Type	Parameter not required here
NPM	Number of coupons remaining (n)
VC	Redemption value of the bond at maturity (R)

Example: A bond with a face value of A bond with a nominal value of $1,000 maturing in 10 years is issued on 15 June 2001. The interest rate is 8% compounded semi-annually. Calculate the price that an investor must pay on 15 June 2001 to obtain a semi-annual rate of return of 6%.

Solution:

The price of the bond on June 15, 2001 corresponds to the present value of the 20 coupons of $40 plus the present value of the redemption of $1,000.Using the function VA (6%; 20; -40; -1000), we find that the price is equal to $770.60.

BIBLIOGRAPHY

❖**The books :**

Curriculum National des Humanités Techniques Commerciales, March 2014;
Jacques LONCHAMP, Introduction aux systèmes informatiques, Paris, Dunod, 2011.

❖**Websites :**

https://www.ionos.fr.
http://www.ordinateur.cchttps://www.arobase.org
https://www.schoolap.com
https://support.microsoft.com
https://www.blog-nouvelles-technologies.fr
https://www.coursinfo.fr

TABLE MATERIAL

MIX
Papier aus verantwortungsvollen Quellen
Paper from responsible sources
FSC® C105338

Printed by Books on Demand GmbH, Norderstedt / Germany